# BEHOLD
# A GREAT LIGHT

*A Daily Devotional for the Nativity Fast
through Theophany*

Fr. Basil Ross Aden
Elissa Bjeletich Davis
Fr. Stephen De Young
Fr. Stephen Freeman
Fr. Michael Gillis
Laura S. Jansson
Nicole M. Roccas
Brandi Willis Schreiber

Edited by Lynnette Horner

ANCIENT FAITH PUBLISHING    CHESTERTON, INDIANA

Published by:
Ancient Faith Publishing
A Division of Ancient Faith Ministries
1050 Broadway, Suite 6
Chesterton, IN 46304

All Old Testament quotations, unless otherwise identified, are
from the Orthodox Study Bible, © 2008 by St. Athanasius
Academy of Orthodox Theology (published by Thomas
Nelson, Inc., Nashville, Tennessee) and are used by permission.
New Testament quotations, unless otherwise identified,
are from the New King James Version of the Bible, © 1982
by Thomas Nelson, Inc., and are used by permission.

Cover detail from the Nativity icon at the Church of the
Nativity, Bethlehem—public domain

ISBN: 978-1-955890-52-6

Library of Congress Control Number: 2023938094

# Contents

# Foreword

The Orthodox faithful begin the journey toward the Birth of Christ with the Nativity fast on November 15—many days before Western Christians commence their Advent preparations on the first of December. It can be a lonely time spiritually. We try our best to fast, give sacrificially, and devote more time to prayer while everyone else seems to be feasting, spending, and hosting parties. And during the fast, the services continue with barely a mention of the Incarnation until the final week before Christmas. At last, the hymnography of the Nativity unfolds, and the Church opens the doors to a treasure house of gifts for believers—gifts of wisdom, of insight, of the Holy Spirit's inspiration. But during that sacred week, most of us are busy with guests, travel, baking, and buying. So these precious gifts often remain unopened, overlooked, and forgotten.

We might search online for books to help us prepare our hearts for Christmas, but nothing quite fits. Catholic Advent devotionals are limited to the first twenty-five days of December, as are the Protestant ones, which do not offer the Virgin

Mary the veneration due to her. And none of them offer the riches of the ancient Church for readers to ponder.

Ancient Faith Publishing is now stepping into this gap with *Behold a Great Light,* a devotional that stretches from the beginning of the fast through the Nativity, and on through the twelve days of Christmas to the Theophany of Our Lord and Savior Jesus Christ. Our contributors in this work of love are Ancient Faith authors, bloggers, and podcasters. They each bring their own unique perspectives to these meditations on the mysteries of the Incarnation. (You can find their biographies in the back of the book.)

These daily meditations mostly follow the chronological order of the events surrounding the Birth of Christ as well as His Baptism, occasionally pausing to include essays honoring the iconography, saints, and sacred events that the fixed feast days commemorate during this season. Each day's entry begins with a passage from Scripture, or occasionally from another ancient writing, and ends with the gift of a hymn from the Church. Because the hymns are arranged topically, they are often out of order in terms of the Orthodox worship cycle. This means that on some days we will open the Church's gifts early to meditate on her beautiful, familiar words—or maybe even discover them for the first time.

This devotional also contains some bonus material for the commemorations that move around on the calendar (such as the Sunday before Nativity: the Commemoration of the Holy Fathers) and for the day after Theophany, when the Synaxis of St. John the Forerunner will encourage us to press onward in the life of faith through the rest of the year.

May *Behold a Great Light* turn your thoughts to Christ, His Mother, the saints, and the mystery of the Incarnation during this holy season.

Lynnette Horner
Editor

# Keeping Vigil

### FR. STEPHEN FREEMAN

*"Lord, now You are letting Your servant depart in peace,*
*According to Your word;*
*For my eyes have seen Your salvation*
*Which You have prepared before the face of all peoples,*
*A light to bring revelation to the Gentiles,*
*And the glory of Your people Israel."*

—LUKE 2:29–32

A story is told of an old monk in the desert who would turn to face the east at sundown each day and continue praying until he saw the sun reappear. Somehow this story has always struck me as more profound than simply saying, "He prayed all night long." For, beyond the fact that he was praying, he was also *waiting*. He was keeping a true vigil in that he was actually watching for something. In the first instance—praying all night—he might develop a happy joy that he was almost finished. That would somehow be wrong. Instead, this unknown monk could welcome with joy the sun's appearance, completely apart from the fact that his nightly prayers were ending. The object of his waiting had appeared, bringing his heart some measure of fulfillment.

1

Forty days before Christmas, the Orthodox Church begins a period of waiting. We change the way we eat—eating less, avoiding certain categories of foods. It can feel like a season of absence, like a labor to be done whether we like it or not. When our hearts sink into such a line of thought, our fast becomes a chore and holds little joy. We find ourselves alone in the desert, forgetting that we're waiting for the sun.

We live in a hurry. Stores promise us "no waiting!" Time spent standing in line or stuck in traffic is seen as wasted. Patience is not something we cultivate as a virtue, and various teachers attack our unhappy wasted time by urging us to learn to live "in the moment." There is, no doubt, something to be said for such a practice. Too often, though, our mindful moments are spent trying to become content with emptiness.

The Nativity fast, like the Lenten fast, is not rightly seen as wasted time—time when we're not yet doing the thing for which we're preparing. It is more like *extended* time, an experience that encompasses weeks of our lives in its unfolding. The Nativity fast is already the Nativity in this sense.

The period of the fast is a period of formation, a time when through our actions and intentions we intensify our desire for Christ and His life within us. We could say of the Mother of God that the Nativity extended through nine months of gestational preparation. In a similar manner, the Christ Child is being "formed within us" as we bear Him in the fast. Saint Paul drew on this image when he called the Galatians "my little children, for whom I labor in birth again until Christ is formed in you" (Gal. 4:19). Our fasting in this season, coupled with our prayers and almsgiving, is part of a formation of Christ within us. The character of Christ is slowly shaped within us to some degree through the working of the Holy Spirit.

Our efforts of waiting, preparing, fasting, praying, and giving alms are not unlike our actions throughout the year. Although the Nativity and Lenten fasts are more rigorous than the Wednesday–Friday fast in most weeks, they are still only fasts. They are rewarded with the joys of a feast when their labors are accomplished. Those joys themselves are but echoes of a greater feast.

The whole of our life can be seen as a fasting period, a time of preparation. Our lives are moving toward the truly Great Feast, the heavenly banquet at the end of the age, or its foretaste in the "homecoming" each of us finds at the end of this life. The small things we learn in the various seasons reflect this long arc of a lifetime. Saint Paul said it well:

> For our light affliction, which is but for a moment, is working for us a far more exceeding *and* eternal weight of glory, while we do not look at the things which are seen, but at the things which are not seen. For the things which are seen *are* temporary, but the things which are not seen *are* eternal. (2 Cor. 4:17–18)

*Your Nativity, O Christ our God,*
*has caused the light of knowledge to rise upon the world.*
*For therein the worshippers of the stars were*
*by a star instructed to worship You,*

*the Sun of Righteousness, and to know*
*You as Orient from on high.*
*Glory to You, O Lord.*
—VIGIL OF GREAT COMPLINE, EVE OF
THE NATIVITY, DECEMBER 24

# *"Follow Me"*

FR. STEPHEN FREEMAN

*Behold, the eyes of the Lord are on those who fear Him,*
*On those who hope in His mercy,*
*To deliver their souls from death*
*And to keep them alive in famine.*
*Our soul shall wait for the Lord;*
*He is our helper and protector;*
*For our heart shall be glad in Him,*
*And we hope in His holy name.*
*Let Your mercy, O Lord, be upon us,*
*As we hope in You.*

—PSALM 32/33:18–22

Today the Church celebrates the Feast of St. Matthew. An ancient tradition assigns his name to the first Gospel, though the text itself never makes mention of its author. Together with the other three evangelists, St. Matthew has acquired a symbol that is often seen in Church iconography and architecture: Matthew is a man or an angel, while Mark is a lion, Luke is an ox, and John is an eagle. These four creatures appear first in the vision of the Prophet Ezekiel (Ezek. 1) and a second time in the Revelation of St. John (chapter 4). Tradition has associated these appearances with the four Gospels.

Saint Matthew is symbolized by the figure of a man because his Gospel focuses on the humanity of Christ, beginning with His genealogy—His human lineage. Some also note that St. Matthew's Gospel often casts Christ as a "New Moses" giving a "new law" in His teaching in the Sermon on the Mount. Of course, his Gospel proclaims the divinity of Christ as well, in harmony with all the Gospels.

Saint Matthew was well situated to see the humanity of Christ. He had been a tax collector when Jesus called him to be an apostle (Matt. 9:9). As such, he would have been despised by his fellow citizens as a sellout to their hated Roman overlords.

There was no particular virtue in being a tax collector. There is no story that encourages us to be sympathetic to such a path in life. We are, however, keenly aware in our time of the separations and pain caused by political differences. Very few Jews, particularly those who were pious, would have felt anything other than hatred for someone who had chosen to side with Rome. It is therefore all the more remarkable that Christ reaches across that divide to call Matthew to Himself.

We have no background for St. Matthew's conversion. We are told simply that he was sitting, doing his work, when Jesus confronted him and said, "Follow Me." Later, Matthew had a feast in his home to which he invited other tax collectors and "sinners," together with Jesus. When the religious leaders of Israel complained about this, Christ said, "Those who are well have no need of a physician, but those who are sick. But go and learn what *this* means: 'I desire mercy and not sacrifice.' For I did not come to call the righteous, but sinners, to repentance" (Matt. 9:12–13).

We can see in this exchange the humanity of Christ, who argues with the religious leaders about the nature and meaning of the Law. In Matthew's Gospel Christ will say, "Do not think that I came to destroy the Law. . . . I did not come to destroy but to fulfill" (5:17). Repeatedly, Christ makes clear that the nature of the Law is found in mercy and generosity.

Saint John's Gospel, where Christ's divinity is most clearly displayed, speaks of transcendent love rather than the Law. Matthew, however, hears in Christ the revelation that the Law of God, rightly understood, is love in the fullness of its truth. No doubt, his movement from tax collector to apostle was a movement toward just such an understanding.

Saint Matthew is not just a tax collector; he is also a symbol of the many sinful things that occupy our time and separate us from God and neighbor. Christ's simple words echo through him to all of us: "Follow Me." It is an invitation to come to Christ, but also to the banquet as though we are in Matthew's home. There we can feast with our fellow sinners, now made righteous through the Blood of Christ, who bids us each to come to His table. What joy!

*O Apostle Matthew,*
*You heard the Voice of the Word and*
*received the light of faith.*

*You abandoned the office of publican*
*and proclaimed Christ God's self-emptying.*
*Ask that those who praise you may receive*
*forgiveness and great mercy.*
—TROPARION OF ST. MATTHEW, NOVEMBER 16

# Grace to Become Small

FR. STEPHEN FREEMAN

*"And you, O Bethlehem, House of Ephrathah, though you are fewest in number among the thousands of Judah, yet out of you shall come forth to me the One to be ruler of Israel. His goings forth were from the beginning, even from everlasting."*

*Therefore He shall give them up until the appointed time for her to give birth, and then the remnant of their brothers will return to the sons of Israel. And He shall stand and see, and shepherd His flock in the strength of the Lord, and they will dwell in the glory of the name of the Lord their God, for now they will be magnified unto the ends of the earth.*

*And she will have peace.*

—MICAH 5:1–4A

Among the most consistent themes in the history of salvation is the place held by small things and weak things, things that are unsuited for the task required of them. Indeed, we get the impression that God prefers to use the most insignificant things to accomplish the things that are truly significant. Saint Paul says it this way:

For you see your calling, brethren, that not many wise according to the flesh, not many mighty, not many noble, *are called.* But God has chosen the foolish things of the world to put to shame the wise, and God has chosen the weak things of the world to put to shame the things which are mighty; and the base things of the world and the things which are despised God has chosen, and the things which are not, to bring to nothing the things that are. (1 Cor. 1:26–28)

We live in a culture that values excellence. We reward it, we applaud it, we make a great display of it for all to admire. We all want to put our best foot forward and to hide those things that we consider weak and broken. It is easy to imagine in our cultural madness that only the strong and talented will be saved.

But the clear pattern of Scripture says quite the opposite. If Bethlehem, a shepherd's town, was the chosen place of the Savior's Birth, then the pattern is repeated as Nazareth ("Can anything good come out of Nazareth?" [John 1:46]) was appointed to be the town forever linked with the name of Jesus. The Supreme Excellence that is God purposefully chose to empty Himself and to identify Himself with the small, weak, and despised. In His choice of Mary, He found a young maiden, a virgin, whose meekness reached heights never before seen. She herself declared:

He has scattered *the* proud in the imagination of their hearts.
He has put down the mighty from *their* thrones,
And exalted *the* lowly.
He has filled *the* hungry with good things,
And *the* rich He has sent away empty. (Luke 1:51–53)

We fail to see that we ourselves are God's Bethlehem, His Nazareth. As much as we tend to despise our own weakness, it is treasured by God. Saint Paul said, "We have this treasure in earthen vessels, that the excellence of the power may be of God and not of us" (2 Cor. 4:7).

We are naturally protective of our weaknesses. They are easily exploited by others and, in a highly competitive culture, place us at a disadvantage. However, those same protective habits have a way of hardening the heart. The psalmist says, "A broken and humbled heart God will not despise" (50/51:19). In light of this, the Church invites us, particularly in seasons of fasting and preparation, to bring ourselves to confession and lay our souls bare, together with our weaknesses and broken places.

This is perhaps the most difficult aspect of the spiritual life. Weakness is, though, the one thing that all of us have in common. Not everyone is strong or talented. Not everyone excels. But even the mightiest and the most gifted have weak places and brokenness. Christ never encourages us to become excellent in the manner that modern culture values. He points us, time and again, toward the poor, the weak, the hungry, and the lonely. He consistently forgives the sinners who ask for help. It is our weakness and our brokenness that unite all of us in our common humanity. Indeed, Christ invites us to find our true humanity in the path of humility.

Our weakness and brokenness are not sin, but they allow us to reveal our sins. That revelation is medicine for the heart. May God give us grace to become small like Bethlehem and to be despised like Nazareth.

11

*Sion, keep festival; Jerusalem, be glad;*
*City of Christ God, receive the Creator,*
*contained in a cave and in a manger.*
*Open to me your gates, and entering by*
*them I shall see swaddled as a babe*
*the One who holds creation in His grasp,*
*whom angels hymn with unceasing voice,*
*the Lord, the Life-giver, who saves our race.*
—VESPERS FOR DECEMBER 2

# Behold a Great Light

FR. STEPHEN FREEMAN

*O country of Zebulun, land of Naphtali, by the way of the sea, and the rest dwelling along the seacoast and parts of Judea, and the land beyond the Jordan, Galilee of the Gentiles, a people who walk in darkness, behold a great light; and you who dwell in the country of the shadow of death, upon you a light will shine.*

—ISAIAH 9:1

The dramatic opening words of Genesis introduce creation with the coming of light: "Then God said, 'Let there be light'" (1:3). This statement is poetic on the one hand and strangely scientific on the other. It establishes from the beginning a tension between light and darkness, between creation and nothingness.

The Fathers of the Church were not physicists, but they had strong intuitions about the nature of light and existence. Following the lead of the Gospels, in which light and life are virtually synonymous, they added to light and life the notions of being and goodness. All these concepts are a way of unpacking the simple statement of Genesis that God saw what He had made and said that it was good. Creation, in the divine intention, is good. It is light and life, being and goodness.

This same understanding can also be seen in the treatment of darkness. In the Gospel of St. John, Christ is described as Light, and we read that "the darkness has not overcome it" (1:5, ESV). Darkness obviously carries natural concerns. It is easier to hide in the darkness and thus easier to obscure evil deeds. Darkness also presents the simple danger of stumbling, of not being able to see where we are going. More than this, however, is what the Fathers saw in the phenomenon of darkness: Darkness is not a thing in itself. It is an *absence*, an emptiness, a place where the light does not shine. Darkness is thus a parasite, in the same way that evil is a parasite of the good. Evil is not a thing but an absence, a misdirection, a refusal of the light.

This kind of darkness is something that inhabits our world in many ways. The darkness of ignorance is an absence of learning and wisdom. A darkness of poverty and hunger occurs in the absence of charity and justice. A darkness of evil thoughts and envy grows when a heart shuts out the light of God's goodness and turns in on itself.

It is into just such a darkness that Christ comes as the Light. In the passage from Isaiah quoted above, the lands where people dwelt in darkness and in the "shadow of death" were lands inhabited by Gentiles, those who had no knowledge of God. These lands are also a metaphor for the whole world. Christ's coming is like a new creation—God speaking into darkness and chaos, "Let there be light!"

This metaphor extends not just to the wider world but to our inner world as well. No matter our background or upbringing, great parts of our lives lie under a cloud of darkness. Even with the most natural good that can be found within a human being, there remains an emptiness. There also remains a fullness that has yet to be seen.

Saint John says of Christ, "[He] was the true Light which gives light to every man coming into the world" (John 1:9). Perhaps we might understand our daily life as an effort to come into the Light. Every prayer we pray, every kind word we speak, every deed of generosity and forgiveness we perform allows the flame of that Light to burn brighter. That Light is the source of our life, the energy that transforms even the hidden places within us and banishes the darkness that lives like a parasite.

Zebulun and Naphtali were lands of the Gentiles, places once considered beyond the reach or concern of Israel. Christ has broken all such limits and called everyone to Himself. He is the Light of the world and of everything in it.

*A great light has shone for the nations:*
*a divine ray has risen for the darkened;*
*Christ the Sun of glory has dawned*
*for those who sat of old in the darkness of death.*
—VESPERS FOR JANUARY 2

# Who Are Your People?

## FR. STEPHEN FREEMAN

*Abraham begot Isaac, Isaac begot Jacob, and Jacob begot Judah and his brothers. . . . David the king begot Solomon by her who had been the wife of Uriah. . . . And Jacob begot Joseph the husband of Mary, of whom was born Jesus who is called Christ.*

—MATTHEW 1:2, 6, 16

My mother's parents lived on a farm that had been in her family for years. Most of the nearby farms had been in various parts of the family for generations. Time and inheritance had divided a once substantial enterprise into scattered small holdings of various relatives—some close, some not. As children we liked to hike across the farms, out past the creek, climbing fences, wandering about. Our trespassing was often found out and would be met with the demand to know, "Who are your people?"

That, of course, elicited a short recounting of my genealogy. I was Arthur Campbell's grandson, one of Nancy Freeman's boys. That always seemed to settle things as we were sent on our way with a word of caution, such as to avoid a bull or a bad dog.

It was, though, the quintessential Southern question: "Who are your people?" Today, with scattered families and grandparents rarely seen apart from holidays, our "people" would have little or no meaning. But once it meant almost everything.

Both St. Matthew and St. Luke take time to tell us about Jesus' "people." The lists (Matthew's first chapter and Luke's third) do not agree in their details, which is neither here nor there. Both, though, root Christ in the families of Israel through the line of David and Abraham. Jesus' genealogy is a firm reminder that His "people" are like our families. There are illustrious characters (a king and several patriarchs) as well as harlots, adulterers, and worse.

My mother was always concerned about the question of our "people." She had a sense that each of us as individuals carried the weight of the family's honor as well as its sins. It was an old-fashioned sentiment but one that carries more theological truth than most might imagine.

Saint Gregory of Nyssa wrote, "Our whole [human] nature, then, extending from the first to the last, is, so to say, one image of Him Who is."[1] Thus, he sees that Adam, whom God created "in His image," is also the whole of humanity, from beginning to end. In becoming the Son of Mary, Christ made us all "His people." Some are kings and priests, some are harlots and thieves. And none of us is truly free of the burden—and the splendor—of the whole.

Our modern individualism likes to tell us that each of us can be anything we want to be. My mother used to tell me that as well. This belief suggests that with the right education and the right effort, we can shape our lives and the world around us to be whatever pleases our heart's deepest desire. Indeed, we are told, "Follow your dreams!"

I think of this as something easily believed by the young but deeply doubted by the old. Those of us who now see our lives in the rearview mirror know that the playing field was tilted from the beginning. We had choices, but they were limited. We could be several things, but not everything. We carry burdens.

The story of our salvation, of Christ coming among us, is that of a God who makes us His people. It means that He has taken on the whole burden of our past, just as He shares with us the whole weight of His glory. It is said that "none of us is saved alone."

Over time, as I look in my morning mirror, I see the face of my father looking back at me. I never thought I favored him when I was young. But now, the old man is unmistakably there. My reflection is a reminder of all that I received from him, just as he received much from those before. I am not utterly unique but just the latest in a long line of my people. And we are now part of a genealogy that includes a God—the good God who is saving us together. Our people are His Church.

*Let us all praise King David, the ancestor of God,*
*for from him came the Virgin stem;*
*from this stem blossomed the flower Christ.*
*And being delivered from corruption,*
*Adam and Eve cry to Him,*
*for He is compassionate!*
—MATINS FOR DECEMBER 28

# God Chooses the Least Expected

### FR. STEPHEN FREEMAN

*Suddenly a messenger of the Lord appeared to her and said: "Anna, Anna, the Lord God has heard your prayer. You will conceive and give birth, and your child will be talked about all over the world." And Anna said, "As the Lord God lives, whether I give birth to a boy or a girl, I'll offer it as a gift to the Lord my God, and it will serve him its whole life." And right then two messengers reported to her: "Look, your husband Joachim is coming with his flocks." You see, a messenger of the Lord had come down to Joachim and said, "Joachim, Joachim, the Lord God has heard your prayer. Get down from there. Look, your wife Anna is pregnant."*

—PROTOEVANGELION OF JAMES 4[2]

One of the most loved books in the Orthodox Church is one that most people have never read. Scholars call it the *Protoevangelion of James*, though it has had many other names over the centuries. It was written in the second century—some think as early as AD 125. It contains stories about the birth and childhood of Mary, as well as many details about her betrothal to Joseph and the Birth of Christ. Though the book lacked the requirements for inclusion in the canonical Scriptures, its popularity in the Church has been persistent.

Most touching is the account of the parents of the Theotokos, Joachim and Anna. They are described as an elderly couple, deeply pious and faithful. However, they never had children. Both saw this as a deep failure, indicative of the absence of God's blessing. Joachim reaches a point of despair. He leaves Anna and goes into the wilderness. There he pitches a tent and begins to fast and pray—for forty days and nights. He says, "I will not go back for food or drink until the Lord my God visits me. Prayer will be my food and drink."

At the same time, Anna enters into deep mourning and refuses to be consoled. An angel breaks the sadness and lamentation of the story by appearing to Joachim and telling him that God has heard his prayer: Anna will conceive a child. An angel speaks to Anna as well with the news that has been given to her husband. The traditional icon of Joachim and Anna shows the elderly couple in a joyful embrace. It represents the moment they are reunited in their mutual joy, visited by the mercy of God.

It has always said much to me that this book holds such an important place in the life of the Church, its stories honored with major feasts. It reminds us that the life of the Church, while rooted in Scripture, also extends to holy and pious tradition. Family stories have a holy value.

The experience of Joachim and Anna echoes earlier stories such as that of Abraham and Sarah, who did not have a child until they were in their nineties. It also reflects our common human experience of helplessness and frustration. As much as we like to imagine ourselves as the masters of our own lives, we discover over time that some things are beyond our control. Modern technology goes to extreme lengths to eliminate obstacles, but usually at great expense and, even then, with frequent failure. We are creatures, not creators.

This understanding goes to the heart of the gospel itself. The Cross appears to be a monumental failure. God comes among us and is arrested, humiliated, and put to a shameful death. Repeatedly, God chooses the least expected people to fulfill His purpose in the world. An old couple, a shepherd boy, a runaway slave, a thief, a prostitute, an enemy of the Church—the list goes on and on.

There is a message for us in this, one meant for every day. Regardless of what seems impossible to us, what seems to exclude us from the Kingdom of God, we are nevertheless not outside God's plan of salvation. Indeed, the things that seem to disqualify us might become the very things through which God saves us and makes use of us in His purpose.

We see a key to this truth in the attitude of Joachim and Anna. Their hearts were broken over their circumstances in life. But in that predicament, they gave themselves over to prayer and cried out to God. We know how their story turned out: they became the parents of the Virgin Mary. That was their unique place in God's work. But they take their place alongside many others who were equally bound by failure and disappointment: "To the Lord in my affliction I cried out, and He heard me!" (Ps. 119/120:1).

*Anna is now no longer barren and nurses the All-Pure One!*
*She rejoices and calls us all to sing a hymn of praise to Christ,*
*she who from her womb gave mankind*
*the only ever-Virgin Mother.*

—KONTAKION FOR THE POST-FEAST OF THE
NATIVITY OF THE MOTHER OF GOD, SEPTEMBER 9

# Mary Dances

FR. STEPHEN FREEMAN

*And the priest received her, and kissed her, and blessed her, say-
ing: The Lord has magnified your name in all generations. In
you, on the last of the days, the Lord will manifest His redemption to the sons of Israel. And he set her down upon the third
step of the altar, and the Lord God sent grace upon her; and
she danced with her feet, and all the house of Israel loved her.*

—PROTOEVANGELION OF JAMES 7[3]

The Protoevangelion of James gives us endearing stories of
the Virgin Mary's childhood. Her parents had promised
that if God gave them a child, they would give the child to the
service of God. They fulfilled this promise in presenting their
daughter to serve among the virgins in the temple. (Recent
research seems to validate that such a ministry existed.)[4] The
passage quoted above describes her reception in the temple by
the priest, who prophesies about the role she will play in the life
of the world.

But the scene quickly shifts to something wonderfully child-
like: Mary dances. In the midst of such a solemn scene, with all
eyes on her, she offers her only gift. She gives God her joy by

dancing in His presence. At age three, she cannot yet offer the words that we will hear in years to come:

> "My soul magnifies the Lord,
> And my spirit has rejoiced in God my Savior.
> For He has regarded the lowly state of His maidservant;
> For behold, henceforth all generations will call me blessed."
>     (Luke 1:46–48)

Instead of words, she offers a dance—eloquent, childish movement to the glory of God.

If ever you have the blessing to travel to Bethlehem, you will find a church built over the place of the manger. It is a side chapel, beloved of Christians throughout the ages. Bethlehem's church is one of the oldest in the Holy Land. But when you get there, you'll discover something strange. The entrance to this great church is a door so small that it can only be entered by stooping over.

The original entrance was much larger. However, during a time of foreign occupation, marauders made a habit of riding their horses into the church to desecrate it and harass the pilgrims. Today, the door is about four feet tall and is known as the Door of Humility.

It seems fitting that the entrance into that wonderful place should require that we "become small" to enter. The entire story of Christ's Nativity, including the barrenness of Joachim and Anna, the innocence of a virgin child and maiden, the requirement to travel during a difficult time of pregnancy only to be turned away from the inn, the Birth in a stable surrounded by feeding animals—all point to the humility of God.

God's actions are surprising to us because we fail to understand that He Himself is humble. None of His actions are out of character. Instead, they reveal to us the very nature of who God is. He is the God who delights in choosing the humble and meek, in dwelling with those who are despised. His actions surprise us and judge us in that we too often give the most honor to the mighty, the excellent, and the rich.

Years ago in my parish, I built a short analogion—a wooden stand—for a children's icon. It stands in the narthex and is quickly adopted by children who are new to the parish. I love to watch them as they enter. Frequently, instead of crossing themselves before kissing the icon—many are too young to have mastered such a thing—they simply hug the icon and plant a loving kiss. Their response seems to me to be of a piece with the Theotokos's dance as she entered the temple: the spontaneous joy of the innocent who have not yet learned to be self-aware or embarrassed.

We do well, no matter our age, to enter the Door of Humility, wherever we find it, and to allow our hearts to dance in the presence of God. He has promised to do great things for us, and through us for others, if we are willing to be small enough to let that happen.

*Let the portal of the God-receiving temple be opened!*
*For today the temple and throne of the King*
*of all is received therein with glory!*

*Joachim brings her forth, dedicating to the Lord*
*her who was chosen by Him to be His Mother.*
—VESPERS FOR THE FEAST OF THE ENTRANCE
OF THE THEOTOKOS, NOVEMBER 21

# Forerunners in Every Generation

LAURA S. JANSSON

*There was in the days of Herod, the king of Judea, a certain
priest named Zacharias, of the division of Abijah. His wife
was of the daughters of Aaron, and her name was Elizabeth.
And they were both righteous before God, walking in all the
commandments and ordinances of the Lord blameless. But
they had no child, because Elizabeth was barren, and they
were both well advanced in years. . . . Now after those days
his wife Elizabeth conceived; and she hid herself five months,
saying, "Thus the Lord has dealt with me, in the days when He
looked on me, to take away my reproach among people."*

—LUKE 1:5–7, 24–25

Today we contemplate the Forerunner's forerunners—that
is, Zacharias and Elizabeth, the parents of St. John the
Baptist.

We call John the Forerunner because he is a path maker,
scoping out the spiritual terrain for Christ in preparation for
His arrival. Quoting from the Hebrew Scripture, John affirms,
"I *am* 'The voice of one crying in the wilderness: Make straight
the way of the LORD'" (John 1:23/Is. 40:3). It's as if he comes in

27

with a grader, forging a level road through the rocky landscape of our hearts so the King of Glory can enter.

Even prophets have parents, and Zacharias and Elizabeth in turn had readied a path for John. Throughout their long marriage, they'd prepared by keeping "all the commandments and ordinances of the Lord blameless" (Luke 1:6), making their shared life a beautiful nest into which, rather unexpectedly in the end, he'd be welcomed. Possibly they taught him the very Isaiah verse he came to fulfill. On difficult days, perhaps they recalled the angel's promise that their son would "be great in the sight of the Lord, and . . . turn many of the children of Israel to the Lord" (Luke 1:15–16).

Zacharias and Elizabeth, too, had their own forerunners. By tradition, Zacharias was the "son of Berechiah," the priest mentioned in Matthew 23:35; Elizabeth was "of the daughters of Aaron," that is, from priestly stock herself (Luke 1:5). But we can be sure that *many* foremothers and forefathers, mostly unknown to us, handed down to Elizabeth and Zacharias not just their genes or priestly lineage but their faith in God. Without a continuous succession of grandparents in their family tree, snuggling little ones close around a courtyard fire to pass on a precious inheritance to each new generation, Elizabeth and Zacharias would never have come to be the parents of the Forerunner. Every single forerunner is indispensable in the journey to this point.

One of Elizabeth's foremothers makes herself known: Elisheba, an ancient namesake who shares Elizabeth's name in Hebrew form. Elisheba beautifully foreshadows and magnifies her descendant's role in Christ's coming into the world twelve centuries later. Though remote from one another in years, the two women are utterly entwined in significance. Like Elizabeth, Elisheba married a priest—Aaron, the first high priest—and had a relative named Miriam (a variant of "Mary"). Elisheba's Miriam helped rescue her brother, the infant Moses, from the river in Egypt to save him from Pharaoh's murder of the Israelite boys; Elizabeth's Mary fled *to* Egypt to protect her son from such a genocide under Herod. Like Elizabeth, Elisheba is present to hear her Mary sing a crowning song of deliverance. As her people walk through the parted waters of the Red Sea, Miriam exults, "Let us sing to the Lord, for He is / greatly glorified. / Horse and rider He cast into the sea" (Ex. 15:21). The New Testament Elizabeth hears those words echo in Mary's song: "My soul magnifies the Lord. . . . He has put down the mighty from *their* thrones, / And exalted *the* lowly" (Luke 1:46, 52).

If the Forerunner's forerunners are so bound to forerunners of their own, I might consider: What of my own spiritual lineage? Who are my forerunners in faith and flesh? Who are those without whom I would never have come to know God? Some feature in frames on my living room walls; others are part of an unseen "cloud of witnesses" (Heb. 12:1). Equally, to whom might I become a forerunner: children and grandchildren, perhaps, but godchildren, friends, and strangers, too—along with their descendants? For whose sake must I keep my hope in God, as others did for me?

The continual forward rolling of spiritual forebears into spiritual descendants doesn't stop with John the Baptist, or with Christ. Even Our Lord Himself is a forerunner, promising us, "I go and prepare a place for you . . . that where I am, *there* you may be also" (John 14:3). In this we glimpse the *telos*, the culmination, of this succession: our salvation. God's desire to bring us into eternal communion with Him is the golden thread linking us back to Elizabeth and Zacharias, binding us to Christ and weaving ahead through every generation to come.

*She that once was barren does today bring*
*forth Christ's Forerunner, John,*
*the culmination and the crown of all the prophets.*
*For when he, in River Jordan, laid his hand*
*on Him whom the prophets preached aforetime,*
*he was revealed as God the Word's forechosen prophet,*
*His mighty preacher, and His Forerunner in grace.*
—KONTAKION FOR THE NATIVITY OF ST.
JOHN THE FORERUNNER, JUNE 24

# More Spacious than the Heavens

LAURA S. JANSSON

*Therefore the Lord Himself will give you a sign: behold, the virgin shall conceive and bear a Son, and you shall call His name Immanuel.*

—ISAIAH 7:14

Overlooking the faithful from the apse behind the altar, the Theotokos peers over the iconostasis. Her hands are raised to the level of her heart in a traditional posture of prayer, as if showing the priest standing below her how it's done. At her core, nestled in concentric rings of red and blue, is the infant Christ, looking a little—just a little—like an unborn baby in one of the educational charts I show my childbirth classes. He is fully clothed and sitting upright, often with a scroll in His hand, a cross-shaped halo around a full head of hair, and an adult expression, whereas the child on the chart is folded into a contortionist's pose, upside-down, and naked. But both the icon and the chart provide a window into the womb, with its luminous layers of flesh and water. In both cases, the child occupies an improbably large proportion of his mother's body.

This is the icon we call the Virgin of the Sign, as in, "the Lord Himself will give you a sign: behold, the virgin shall conceive." These words of the Old Testament prophet, writing around seven centuries before the birth of Christ, foreshadow how the God of Israel, whose Name could not be spoken and whose face could not be looked upon, would become Jesus of Nazareth, a person with a moniker, a hometown, and a face for His mother to gaze upon. Entering His creation through human flesh, He is Immanuel, "God with Us," in every corner of human experience: in dependency, joy, exile, skinned knees, poverty, celebration, bereavement, hunger, worship, pain, sleep, mockery, bleeding, friendship, loneliness, anger, criminal conviction, and death throes. He is God in the womb, and in the Tomb, and everything in between.

All this is possible only because a young woman, perhaps fourteen years old, agreed to welcome Him into her body. The Church proclaims Mary as Theotokos, a title affirmed in the face of controversy at the fifth-century Council of Ephesus, meaning "the one who gave birth to God." Let's pause to let this sink in, as much as it may. She isn't simply the Mother of God (*Meter tou Theou*), or the God-bearer (*Theophoros*—a title bestowed on other saints), but the one through whose body God emerged into the world. She is the one who contained the infinite God in the small enclosure of her womb, making it "more spacious than the heavens" (*Platytera ton Ouranon*, an alternative name for this icon). Through the most humble and intimate of instruments—a woman's blood, uterus, pelvis, amniotic fluid, umbilical cord, and placenta—the Creator is embedded into the lining of His creation. As St. Ephrem the Syrian marvels, "While the fetus of the Son was being formed in the womb, He Himself was forming babes in the womb" (Nativity Hymn 4).

In offering Him the welcome of her body, Mary also consents to bring Christ into the heart of her existence. Standing there before us, arms raised in prayer and belly full of baby, she demonstrates how to turn our whole lives over as an offering to God. Her pregnant womb, where God found a home, is the symbol of our hearts, where we too can give Him a home. As the Theotokos was for nine months and then a lifetime, we *are* His home (Heb. 3:6).

The Virgin of the Sign seems to say to us: you can do this, too. So as the Liturgy culminates, the priest below raises his arms as she does, chanting, "Let us lift up our hearts!" And we reply, "We lift them up unto the Lord."

*Mary, why are you amazed and awed*
*by what was done in you?*
*And she answers, "For in time I have*
*brought forth a timeless Son.*
*But I have no understanding of His conception.*
*Husbandless am I: how can I bear a son?*
*Who has ever seen seedless childbirth?*
*But where God wills, the order found in*
*nature is overcome, as it is written."*
*So Christ was born from the Virgin*
*Maiden, in Bethlehem of Judea.*
—MATINS FOR THE NATIVITY OF CHRIST, DECEMBER 25

# Making Room for the Christ Child

LAURA S. JANSSON

*Then the angel said to her, "Do not be afraid, Mary, for you have found favor with God. And behold, you will conceive in your womb and bring forth a Son, and shall call His name* JESUS. *He will be great, and will be called the Son of the Highest; and the Lord God will give Him the throne of His father David. And He will reign over the house of Jacob forever, and of His kingdom there will be no end." . . . Then Mary said, "Behold the maidservant of the Lord! Let it be to me according to your word." And the angel departed from her.*

—LUKE 1:30–33, 38

Today we ponder an event that the Church commemorates on March 25, nine months to the day before Christ's Nativity: the conception of the Son of God in the womb of a young woman, Mary. Though, chronologically, this is the seventh great feast of the liturgical year, the festal troparion describes this day as "the beginning of our salvation" because it is the day the Son of God becomes the Son of Man. Putting on the robe of humanity from the Theotokos, the eternal God becomes flesh and dwells among us (John 1:14). "The Lord is king and has put on glorious apparel," we sing in the vesperal prokeimenon of Saturday evening (Ps. 92/93:1). The majestic robe of Christ's flesh will be revealed to the world at the time of His Birth, but from the Annunciation it is now already present, hidden inside His mother's womb.

Consenting to have God conceived in her is the beginning rather than the end of Mary's work. It's not as if, having extracted a satisfactory answer, God has no further need of her. It is the scandal of the Incarnation that the Almighty makes Himself subject to our humanity, even unto death at our hands on a criminal's cross. The Theotokos bears the weight of His dependency, both inside her womb and throughout her life.

During pregnancy, His physical survival will be contingent on her body's functions, the one vein and two arteries of an umbilical cord connecting the Source of all life to the life source of her womb. Other women, when they are pregnant, may meticulously avoid certain foods, such as unpasteurized cheese and deli meats. Imagine the care with which the Theotokos guarded her growing belly! "You received in your womb the Logos," the Salutations to the Theotokos Akathist proclaims; "you held in your arms the One who holds all things. With your milk you nourished Him who with a nod nourishes the entire universe." Glory to God for her faithfulness in feeding Him every time He was hungry.

The sacrifice she makes does not stop at morning sickness and an aching lower back but continues throughout her life. As most mothers do, she devotes not only her body but her entire being to raising her child, singing Him back to sleep at 3 AM, untying the strap of his sandal (see John 1:27), soothing His skinned knees, and baking bread for the Bread of Life. It is a debt of no glib gratitude we owe her for every time she carried Him without stumbling, for each trip to the synagogue and every prayer said at home.

Unlike other mothers, though, the Theotokos also becomes her Son's follower along a difficult path. For His sake she bears the slights of neighbors mistaking an unwed mother's faithfulness for waywardness; she accepts that, after all she has done for Him, *any* one of us who obeys the Word is Christ's mother or brother (see Luke 8:19–21). A sword pierces her heart as she joins the procession to Golgotha, where His horrifying death seems to reverse the natural order by which she should predecease Him, and to undo all the work they have done together.

And yet she retains her hope in Him. Then she is witness to His glorious Resurrection, bringing joy to all the earth and becoming the revered spiritual mother to the Church, despite her aversion to the spotlight. All this work was necessary for God's purposes to be manifest in the world.

This is the lifelong reality to which she consents at this moment of Annunciation. Her uterus, as it now begins to swell with its growing guest, will come to occupy a greater and greater space inside her body. Her own internal organs will, as in any pregnancy, be displaced to make room for her child—her lungs, bladder, and intestines finding space where they may. It is, quite literally, a self-emptying undertaking. With St. John the Forerunner, Mary might say of her growing baby, "He must increase, but I must decrease." Her womb is an icon of what is happening in her life when she agrees self-sacrificially to welcome God, in order that He can come into the world. She turns over her body, her life, her existence to make His life and our salvation possible. Let this be an example to us all.

> *The pre-eternal Mind appointed you as*
> *a secondary light, O Gabriel,*
> *which has illumined all the universe*
> *with divine communications,*
> *revealing to us the truly divine and great mystery*
> *which was hidden from before the ages,*
> *of Him who, though incorporeal,*
> *was incarnate in the Virgin's womb and became man,*
> *that He might save man.*
> —VESPERS FOR THE CONCEPTION OF
> THE THEOTOKOS, DECEMBER 8

# Contemplating the Annunciation Icon

### LAURA S. JANSSON

*And having come in, the angel said to her, "Rejoice, highly favored one, the Lord is with you; blessed are you among women!"*

—LUKE 1:28

Today, let's explore the event of the Annunciation by contemplating its festal icon.

This icon is important because it not only portrays a historical moment—the fluttering ribbons on Gabriel's headband frozen in time—it also reveals a mystery into which we may enter daily. By means of the traditional placement of the Annunciation icon on the Royal Doors, through which the Body of Christ passes during the Great Entrance of every Divine Liturgy, the very fabric of the church building shows the reality: as Christ enters the world through the door of His Mother's flesh, so He enters the world through our own very real, physical, and practical lives, offered up to Him in a sacrifice of thanksgiving.

From the top of the icon, we see a heavenly light descend, sometimes shown splitting into three rays to indicate the presence of the Holy Trinity. In Jesus' conception, the eternal Son of God comes to earth, and the ray reaches toward Mary, an ordinary young person who has "found favor" with God. On its way, this ray passes through a scarlet cloth suspended above the scene. In iconography, overhead drapes indicate indoor events, but here the color of the drape also invokes the human flesh—blood, sinews, muscles, and bones—in which God clothes Himself. Mary is not becoming the Mother of God in just a spiritual or figurative sense, but in sheer biological fact.

Next our eye is caught by the angel who has just swooped in. Gabriel's powerful wings are not yet folded away, and his feet, shod in traveler's sandals, have barely touched the ground. We can almost hear robes swish as he reaches for a connection with Mary. His face seeks eye contact. His right hand gestures forth, part salute, part blessing. His other hand grasps a rod that is both the scepter of authority and the staff for a long journey.

Mary's hands also are telling. From the earliest depictions, she holds a spindle wound with crimson thread, showing that the Theotokos is becoming "the loom of the flesh" on which the Son of God is woven.[5] Mary is a human creature, woven by God within her own mother's womb (Psalm 138/139); with her *yes*, the woven one begins the work of weaving the Weaver. This depiction of Mary weaving has solid historical precedent. The yarn basket sometimes shown spilling at her feet is "the Virgin's basket": Martyr Antoninus records that he venerated it during a sixth-century pilgrimage to the Holy Land. Moreover, according to Protoevangelion 10 (about AD 145), the young Mary was chosen to spin thread for the temple veil, which hung before the Holy of Holies as our Royal Doors hang before the altar.

The young woman spinning evokes an earlier figure: Eve, the first woman. Eve also appears in some icons as a spinner, busy making cloth to cover her nakedness after the Fall. The spinning that began in Mary's womb unravels that Fall, bringing God into humankind so that humankind can be brought into God. "Hail, redemption of the tears of Eve!" we sing to the Theotokos in the Orthros kontakion.

As well as pointing backward to our first mother, Mary's spindle gestures ahead to the Crucifixion, sometimes appearing with an overlapping distaff to form a cross. Indeed, the very temple veil that Mary is spinning for will be "torn in two from top to bottom" upon her son's death (Matt. 27:51). Already present from the conception of Christ is the reality of His utterly self-emptying love.

Next, our eyes pass over to the Theotokos herself. She recoils from the angel's invitation. Her defensive right hand expresses discernment, but perhaps she also holds at arm's length the joyful sorrow that her decision will entail. Nevertheless, she inclines her head toward Gabriel, entering into dialogue with him, willing to countenance his message. Mary's head, bowing humbly, contrasts with the surrounding trappings: the throne-like chair with grand pillars, the podium, and the ruby slippers so unlike Gabriel's footwear. You wouldn't know it to look at her, but she is the one "incomparably more glorious than the seraphim"—yes, even than that gallant archangel there.

Finally, her eyes return to us as we gaze upon her. She looks out, as if asking, "And you? You too have found favor with God. Will you also have Christ be born in you?"

*Open to me the gates of the light who was*
*conceived from your womb, O all-pure,*
*that I may see the ray with triple light of the Godhead,*
*and glorify you, the Sovereign Lady filled with light.*
—MIDNIGHT OFFICE FOR DECEMBER 29

# Prayer in the Shadowlands

LAURA S. JANSSON

*And the angel answered and said to her, "The Holy Spirit will come upon you, and the power of the Highest will overshadow you; therefore, also, that Holy One who is to be born will be called the Son of God. Now indeed, Elizabeth your relative has also conceived a son in her old age; and this is now the sixth month for her who was called barren. For with God nothing will be impossible."*

—LUKE 1:35–37

The Archangel Gabriel's message in today's reading is repeated throughout Scripture and parroted by many a televangelist: with God, nothing will be impossible. "All things *are* possible to him who believes" (Mark 9:23). "Ask, and it will be given to you" (Matt. 7:7). And we should take Christ absolutely seriously. There are indeed times when we perceive an answer to our prayers clearly and immediately, but often this simply isn't the case. When we've been praying for something, seemingly fruitlessly, for ages, we can get rather cynical about mountains, mustard seeds, and the like.

When we hear how the impossible becomes a reality for Ss. Zacharias and Elizabeth, we mustn't forget the backstory. Though we know them as the parents of St. John the Forerunner, they spent most of their lives childless, with no idea whether their prayers for a child would ever be answered. Each monthly cycle, each passing year, must have seemed a deeper confirmation that it wasn't to be. Once Elizabeth entered menopause, they surely reconciled themselves to the answer "no." This holy couple has much to teach us about life in the shadowlands, where God meets our prayers with silence.

It's an uncomfortable place to inhabit. Over time, Zacharias and Elizabeth surely started doubting themselves. They were both from priestly families. They'd done everything by the book and were entirely "blameless." (Now, who else can say that?) Perhaps, they thought, some hidden sin rendered them unfit for God's blessing. Living in a culture that considered infertility a sign of moral failure can't have made things easier. The evangelist has to reassure even the reader that there's nothing wrong with them: "They were both righteous before God . . . But they had no child" (Luke 1:6–7).

Worse than self-doubt, often when God doesn't give us what we want when we want it, we can start doubting Him, too. Perhaps He doesn't really love us, we muse, or perhaps He isn't *there*. And then we're surprised to get a response. Zacharias was a priest and, at that, a priest selected to serve at the temple's altar of incense, where he could surely expect to encounter holiness. Yet he was astonished and afraid to find there an answer to his prayer.

God's response to the holy couple is thoroughly surprising—both more abundant and more challenging than they'd envisaged. It's more abundant in the sense that in giving them a child, God heals them not only of their childlessness but also of their spiritual barrenness, which conflated childlessness with unworthiness. They are not only given a son; they're given a son whom Gabriel names *John*, meaning "God is gracious." This name declares that God's favor is an unearned gift. It isn't when Zacharias and Elizabeth finally "deserve" it that He answers their prayers. Rather, they're given a child because *John*—God is gracious. With the question of their worthiness put aside, Zacharias and Elizabeth are free to receive God's love without the interference of their pride.

But they also get more than they bargained for in the harder sense. Elizabeth receives her husband home from his week's temple service dumb as a doorknob and reduced to wild gesticulation to convey what he has experienced. For her, the silence of his vocal cords is added to the silence of God in the face of their prayer, like insult to injury. It seems to be a punishment for Zacharias's disbelief, "because you did not believe my words" (Luke 1:20).

But his muteness becomes a prophetic sign—a manifestation of the truth of the angel's message, offering Mary hope that *her* faith in Gabriel's message will prove equally warranted (Luke 1:36). Zacharias's silence also creates a still space in his heart, in which he can grow in love toward Elizabeth, John, and God. Finally, Zacharias's silence will prove the path to his martyrdom. Various accounts of his death exist, but tradition identifies him as the Zachariah murdered in front of the temple altar (Matt. 23:35). Herod's soldiers came seeking the life of the infant boys of Israel, and when Zacharias refused to reveal John's whereabouts, they stabbed him to life-giving death.

When our own prayers are answered with pained silence, may it be a silence as fruitful as Zacharias's, which God uses to bring the impossible into existence.

> *Walking in the commandments of the*
> *Lord, O most glorious Elizabeth,*
> *You had unfeigned love for God and*
> *unfeigned love for your neighbor.*
> *And, lo! the fruit of your faith was made reality.*
> *Wherefore, holding festival, we call you blessed.*

—VESPERS FOR ZACHARIAH AND ELIZABETH, SEPTEMBER 5

# "Fiat": Let It Be

LAURA S. JANSSON

*Then Mary said, "Behold the maidservant of the Lord! Let it be to me according to your word." And the angel departed from her.*

—LUKE 1:38

*His mother said to the servants, "Whatever He says to you, do it."*

—JOHN 2:5

We don't really *do* obedience anymore," advised the teachers' trainer when I asked her counsel on working with a particularly spirited student in my Sunday school class. My question felt like a pressing one: how could I model a guiding but uncoercive love for this ebullient eight-year-old when I was at my wits' end? The trainer's skeptical nod said that if I expected compliance or cooperation from my charge, I might as well give up and go back to the 1950s where I belonged.

Amid a society that doesn't really *do* obedience anymore, we struggle to grasp the radical obedience of the Theotokos. In becoming the Mother of God, we assume, she is just doing what she is being told—or, worse, being told what she is doing. We call the event from today's reading the *Annunciation*, as if Mary is the object of a news flash. Archangel Gabriel is reduced to a kind of intrusive singing telegram and the merciful God to an imperious foister of chaos on unsuspecting young virgins.

We forget that the Theotokos could have said no. Like any of us—any young person, in particular!—she had her free will to use as she determined. God's respect for her freedom is so complete that He makes His eternal plan contingent on her answer to His proposal. It is not in His nature to coerce her, because He is Love engaging her with love, and love is only offered freely. He offers to be God with Us but waits at the door to be invited in, never forcing His way. As St. Philaret of Moscow preaches, "The incarnation of the Son of God is . . . not only proclaimed by the sovereign will of the Lord, but also awaits the assent of His handmaid."[6]

Of course, in His timeless omniscience, God knows the Theotokos *will* say yes. We, too, know how the story goes, how (spoiler alert!) this young woman's answer fundamentally alters the course of salvation history. But in our impoverished familiarity with the plot line, we read past the details underlining the true suspense of the moment. This is far from a done deal. Mary is troubled. She has reservations. She pauses to consider logistical questions. It certainly would be easier to decline. A mere wave of her hand can return her to the path she's envisaged for herself: an undramatic family life with a pious carpenter husband, a few stepchildren, and perhaps a couple of their own. One degree of difference separates two entirely different futures.

So, at this moment on a particular day in first-century Palestine, all creation holds its breath. The breeze hesitates at the window. The dropped spindle swings from its thread. The universe hangs in balance, awaiting a single word from a teenager.

When it comes, her word is *yes*: *fiat*, in the Latin of the fourth-century Vulgate Bible. *Let it be.* But even now she is not simply shrugging and saying, "Whatever! Fine!" Her fiat conveys not flaccid compliance, but explosive creativity. The Scriptures place this same word in the mouths of various individuals, none of whom you'd accuse of passivity: Moses, the devil, and St. Paul. Most strikingly, God Himself speaks fiat in the beginning: *Fiat lux*, "Let there be light." With God's fiat, creation springs from utter nothingness into being. With Mary's fiat, a new creation is now underway.

The humble obedience of the Mother of God makes her not a pushover but a victorious warrior-queen, leading the Christian people into the spiritual battle against the enemy. Fiat, from her mouth, is a loud rallying cry rather than an acquiescent sigh. In a world that misunderstands, her example is a powerful corrective, revealing that obedience is more than simply doing what we're told, despite ourselves. It's a free act of cooperation, in which we work in synergy with God as our lives are molded into the shape of His life-giving love.

> *O new wonder, greater than all the wonders of old!*
> *For who has known of a mother who gave*
> *birth without knowing man,*
> *and who has borne upon her arm Him*
> *who fashioned all creation?*

*It has been the will of God to be born.*
*O all-pure one, who has borne Him as a babe in your arms*
*and has maternal boldness before Him:*
*do not cease to pray on behalf of those who honor you,*
*that He take pity and save our souls.*

—GREAT VESPERS, SUNDAY BEFORE CHRISTMAS

# The Spark of Recognition

### LAURA S. JANSSON

*Now Mary arose in those days and went into the hill country with haste, to a city of Judah, and entered the house of Zacharias and greeted Elizabeth. And it happened, when Elizabeth heard the greeting of Mary, that the babe leaped in her womb; and Elizabeth was filled with the Holy Spirit. Then she spoke out with a loud voice and said, "Blessed are you among women, and blessed is the fruit of your womb! But why is this granted to me, that the mother of my Lord should come to me? For indeed, as soon as the voice of your greeting sounded in my ears, the babe leaped in my womb for joy. Blessed is she who believed, for there will be a fulfillment of those things which were told her from the Lord."*

—LUKE 1:39—45

"Why is it granted to *me?*" Elizabeth asks, full of wonder that she is privy to the secret of Christ's Incarnation before it is revealed to the world. We might ask the same question, for the Scripture lets us in on it, too. Saint Luke's narrative gives us a window into an intimate encounter that is hidden from the world. It takes place in the hills, where Elizabeth is concealing an unexpected pregnancy. With her temporarily mute husband for company, she shelters in quietude, protected from the idle speculation of those who don't comprehend. Into her seclusion, Elizabeth welcomes her young relative Mary, arriving on women's business.

From this most private moment will come two of the Church's most widely repeated hymns, proclaimed in public down the ages: Elizabeth's greeting, "Blessed *are* you among women, and blessed *is* the fruit of your womb!" (Luke 1:42), and Mary's Magnificat, "My soul magnifies the Lord, / and my spirit has rejoiced in God my Savior. . . ." (Luke 1:46–55).

But for now the evangelist zooms in still closer, allowing us a glimpse inside the bodies of these women. We see that Mary also carries a quiet miracle as she walks into Elizabeth's room: the tiny, even less mature, pregnancy in her own womb. As she approaches, there's a spark of recognition. The infant John, veiled inside his mother's flesh, identifies the infant Christ veiled inside His, and leaps in exuberant joy. Given that this was Elizabeth's sixth month, when most first-time mothers start to feel the initial flutters of their baby's movements, perhaps this was her quickening. And what a quickening! She knew in theory that John would be "filled with the Holy Spirit, even from his mother's womb" (Luke 1:15), but it was surely another thing altogether to feel the jolt of it through her own body.

Elizabeth cries out, and at first Mary may not know what to make of her cry. Elizabeth's pregnancy is unforeseen but yearned for throughout a long marriage at the heart of their community; Mary's is unforeseen and apparently a death knell for her nascent life with Joseph and her place in adult society. This pregnancy could be an actual death knell too: the Theotokos must have feared she'd be stoned for her imputed misdeeds. She may have been prepared to hear a cry of alarm and chastisement from her relative Elizabeth, a priest's wife. How comforting, then, to be met instead with a cry of joy and recognition.

This recognition between John and Christ, Elizabeth and Mary, mirrors the recognition of God, who, as the Liturgy of St. Basil puts it, "knows the name and age of each, even from his mother's womb." As someone who has been blessed to carry five babies and to work alongside women as they carry many more, I know each pregnancy is different. Even from the womb, every person somehow conveys a distinct spirit, identity, pattern of relationships, and ministry in the world. Without exception, God calls *each one* of us to a vocation belonging to no one else in history.

John is clearly a prophet from the womb. His identity is fully established, yet during Elizabeth's pregnancy we must wait for it to be more fully revealed at his birth, and to come to fruition in his ministry. This waiting to see face to face what is already seen through a glass, darkly, is the eschatological labor of pregnancy. It offers an icon of the spiritual waiting we do in the life of faith. The Kingdom of God is at hand—it is within us—and yet we yearn for it to come in fullness. Now is the time of our salvation, yet we have to wait to become what we truly are.

In this time of fruitful waiting, Elizabeth and Mary will walk together through their pregnancies, edifying one another for the difficult road ahead. Their conceptions being three months apart, the physical needs of their respective trimesters dovetail beautifully together. Elizabeth is there for Mary's nauseating first trimester, and Mary will be there for Elizabeth's exhausting third. As well as practical help, there must also have been a deeper sustenance in their kinship, providing the supportive spiritual environment in which St. John and Christ are being formed. Whenever Mary questions her future during the coming nine months, she can turn her eyes to her cousin's belly and remember Gabriel's words: with God, everything is possible.

*O Prophet and Forerunner of the presence of Christ,*
*we who fervently honor you cannot worthily praise you.*
*For by your revered and glorious birth*
*the barrenness of your mother and the*
*muteness of your father were unbound,*
*and the incarnation of the Son of God*
*is proclaimed to the world.*

—APOLYTIKION FOR THE NATIVITY OF THE
FORERUNNER AND BAPTIST JOHN, JUNE 24

# He Has Bowed the Heavens

### FR. BASIL ROSS ADEN

And Mary said:
"My soul magnifies the Lord,
And my spirit has rejoiced in God my Savior.
For He has regarded the lowly state of His maidservant;
For behold, henceforth all generations will call me blessed.
For He who is mighty has done great things for me,
And holy is His name.
And His mercy is on those who fear Him
From generation to generation.
He has shown strength with His arm;
He has scattered the proud in the imagination of their hearts.
He has put down the mighty from their thrones,
And exalted the lowly.
He has filled the hungry with good things,
And the rich He has sent away empty.
He has helped His servant Israel,
In remembrance of His mercy,
As He spoke to our fathers,
To Abraham and to his seed forever."

—LUKE 1:46–55

The hymn selected for today declares that "He has bowed the heavens and come down to live with men." In this mystery is the foundation of our salvation, for all that the Lord Jesus Christ has done for us depends on this greatest of all events in history, His Incarnation.

"He bowed the heavens." To bow is to make oneself lower than what we honor. Even so, the Lord in His Incarnation lowered the heights of His dwelling place. By coming to live with us, He brought heaven to earth. Now the dwelling place of God is the womb of a Virgin Mother, and by her the Lord of heaven comes to make earth His home.

What is the key to this astounding act of self-abasement? It is humility. As St. Paul says, "He humbled Himself and became obedient *to the point of* death" (Phil. 2:8). Humility is the way God works in our world. He descends to earth so we might ascend to heaven. He humbles Himself so we might be exalted. He becomes man so that we might become like God by grace through the working of the Holy Spirit in us (Phil. 2:13).

The story of our salvation begins with humility—not only the Lord's, but Mary's. The Virgin Mary does not become the Mother of God because she is strong, rich, famous, or honorable. To be a maidservant of the Most High, she must be lowly. Therefore, she sets aside her will to say, "Let it be to me according to your word" (Luke 1:38).

Saint Isaac the Syrian writes, "Mysteries are revealed to the humble."[7] Accordingly, in her humility, Mary grasps the mystery of the Lord's works for our salvation. She sings in her Magnificat that the Lord lifts up the lowly. He strengthens the weak.

He feeds the hungry. He makes the poor rich. He gives children to the barren. He lifts up those who are fallen.

But the mighty have no need for the Lord's strength. The rich and satisfied have no desire for the grace of God. The fruitful can rely on their own abilities. But in the end, as Mary says, the Lord, who might have been their helper, casts them down in their conceit.

Humility, therefore, is a central virtue for our observance of this Nativity fast. In this season, we worship the Almighty for the greatness of His humility. We magnify the Mother of God for the excellence of her lowliness. And in the wonder of our contemplation of the Lord's works of mercy, we find humility, as St. Isaac teaches.

It is appropriate that we celebrate the hope of the Lord's Incarnation with fasting, confession, and prayer. For fasting applies humility to the body. Repentance applies humility to the soul. And our prayers apply humility to our need for God. Thus we control our bodily appetites that we may be spiritually filled. We confess our sins that we may be cleansed. We pray for God's mercy that we may be freed of every desire but knowing God.

The Lord has "bowed the heavens and come down" that He might bring us up with Him to heaven. And the Virgin Mary has become the handmaid of the Lord in her lowly estate. Likewise, we are called to "let this mind be in you which was also in Christ Jesus" (Phil. 2:5), who left His throne of glory to share the lowliness of our human nature. And so we reflect on the promise of St. Isaac the Syrian: "Every man who has been clothed with [humility] has truly been made like unto Him Who came down from His own exaltedness, and hid the splendor of His majesty, and concealed His glory with humility."[8]

*Who among men understands the depth of*
*the wisdom and knowledge of God?*
*Who among the wise can explain the*
*abyss of God's love for mankind?*
*He has bowed the heavens and come down to live with men,*
*the Lord whom all creation blesses and*
*glorifies throughout all the ages.*
—VESPERS FOR DECEMBER 22

# Ready to Respond

FR. BASIL ROSS ADEN

*And Jesus, walking by the Sea of Galilee, saw two brothers,
Simon called Peter, and Andrew his brother, casting a net into
the sea; for they were fishermen. Then He said to them, "Follow Me, and I will make you fishers of men." They immediately left their nets and followed Him. Going on from there,
He saw two other brothers, James the son of Zebedee, and
John his brother, in the boat with Zebedee their father, mend-
ing their nets. He called them, and immediately they left the
boat and their father, and followed Him.*

—MATTHEW 4:18–22

It happens often. A patient lies in a coma in the ICU. Her
loved ones visit and pray fervently for some sign of hope. Days
go by. Then one morning, they see the beginning of the answer
to their prayers: a small but noticeable response, an indication
that their loved one is waking up and beginning to recover.

Touching incidents like this show that the root of human
relationships is responsiveness: from birth, a baby responds to
touch, then to facial expressions, then to smiles, and then to
speech. So it is with our relationship to God. We are created to

respond to our God, and as we do so, we grow in our closeness to our Creator and Redeemer.

Today we celebrate the feast day of St. Andrew, the first who responded to the Lord's call. He opened his heart to the Lord twice. The first time was in the desert beyond the Jordan, when John the Baptist pointed to Jesus as the "Lamb of God" (John 1:35–40). And the second time was on the shore of Lake Galilee, when Andrew left his nets to follow the Lord as His disciple (Mark 1:16–18).

How much joy the Lord must feel when His creation responds to Him as Andrew, the "First-Called," did. His exultation is more than the joy of finding a lost sheep or the relief of recovering a lost coin (Luke 15:1–10). It is more than the elation we feel when a loved one is revived from unconsciousness. Like the father of the prodigal son (Luke 15:20), the merciful God waits for the smallest sign, the tiniest indication, the briefest signal that we are ready to respond to Him. For when we respond, then we can begin to get to know Him. And when we continue to respond to Him, we grow in grace until our whole lives are a total response to His love and mercy.

As we observe the Nativity fast, we consider that the responsiveness of St. Andrew reminds us of the greater receptiveness of the Virgin Mary. She was not forced against her will to be the Mother of God. Everything depended on her willing response to the message. Mary answered the greatest divine call with the greatest response ever made to the Almighty.

In this season of prayer and fasting, we might consider what is preventing us from responding to the Lord as Andrew and the Virgin Mary did. If we are spiritually asleep, from what do we need to be awakened? If we are drowsy with worldly distractions, what would rouse us to heavenly concerns? If we are living a bad dream of worries, troubles, and cares, what would free us from this nightmare?

As our souls slumber, the Lord stands beside us, and just as He called Andrew and the Virgin Mary, He gently calls us. Will we stir at the sound of His voice? Will we open our hearts to His loving touch? Will we open our eyes to the vision of Christ, who loved us so much that He came down from heaven to be born of a Virgin Mother?

What does such responsiveness require? Only "faith and obedience," as St. John Chrysostom teaches.[9] The Virgin Mary trusted the angel's message, as astonishing as it was (Luke 1:29). Having heard her calling, she accepted it with obedience. And St. Andrew trusted the summons of the Lord Jesus even though He had not yet performed any miracle. Immediately the first disciple obeyed the Word of Christ.

In this Nativity fast, the voice of God is calling us to forsake every worldly concern and to follow Him. Responsiveness is the beginning as well as the end of discipleship. Once we awaken to the Lord's call, He can lead us step by step into a closer and deeper relationship with Him. Finally, if we continue to respond to the Lord, as St. Andrew and the Mother of God did, we will fully awaken to the eternal life of the resurrection.

*Having been the disciple of Him that*
*sprang forth from a barren woman,*
*the teacher of piety and chastity, who*

*showed the way to purity,*
*when the Offspring of the Virgin shone forth,*
*then were you a most fervent lover of*
*virtue, O blessed Andrew,*
*and, making ascent within your heart,*
*you were caught up from glory to the*
*ineffable glory of Christ our God.*
*Him you beseech that He save and enlighten our souls.*

—VESPERS FOR ST. ANDREW, NOVEMBER 30

# Untying the Knot

### FR. BASIL ROSS ADEN

*Then Mary said, "Behold the maidservant of the Lord! Let it be to me according to your word."*

—LUKE 1:38

For the sake of ambition, Lady Macbeth has murdered the king. Now she cannot wash away his blood. She roams the castle sleepwalking, wringing her hands and mumbling, "What is done cannot be undone."

Whatever we have done cannot be taken back. That is the principle that has kept the human race in bondage. We cannot undo what Eve, the mother of the human race, has done, and we are held fast in the chains of death and corruption as a consequence of her sin.

The hymn for today's meditation declares our release from this captivity: "Because of the malady of disobedience, Eve received the curse within herself. But you, O Virgin Theotokos, have blossomed forth the blessing to all the world." With the Church we reflect today on this incredible reversal of our former bondage, an undoing that promises freedom from the tyranny of the past.

Our hymn points to two spiritual mothers. These matriarchs are the heads of two orders: the way of slavery and death, and the order of freedom and life. The first mother is the old Eve, who ate of the forbidden fruit in the Garden of Eden. Adam called her Eve, that is, "Life," "because she was the mother of all living" (Gen. 3:20). And yes, she is our primal ancestor. But she, in fact, is the mother of death, for by her disobedience, she gave birth to sin and death.

The other mother is the Virgin Mary, who gave birth to the Son of God. This new Eve is the Mother of Life, because as a result of her obedience, the human race was restored to the promise of eternal life. Speaking of her, the early Church Father St. Irenaeus (about 130–202) wrote, "The knot of Eve's disobedience was loosed by the obedience of Mary. For what the virgin Eve had bound fast through unbelief, this did the virgin Mary set free through faith."[10]

As we reflect on this marvelous undoing of what was done, we consider the difference between these two ways of being. The story of Eve in Genesis is troubling. The consequences of the sin of Eve and Adam are eviction from the Garden of Paradise and condemnation outside its gates. Our hymn says, "Because of the malady of disobedience, Eve received the curse within herself." What curse? The disfavor of God, which was the inevitable consequence of the disobedience, the "ancestral sin" of Adam and Eve (Rom. 5:18).

In this light, the blessing that undoes the curse that Eve received means much more to us. Our hymn says, "You, O Virgin Theotokos, have blossomed forth the blessing to all the world." By the One whom the new Eve bore into the world, the ancient curse is annulled. We are no longer sentenced to death but given the blessing of eternal life.

What joy, what peace, what comfort! What a reason to magnify the honor of the Virgin. Her obedience was the pivot point in the course of history. How can we help but amplify her praises, even as we worship the Savior who came into the world through the gate of His human Mother?

With profound thanksgiving and devotion, we, the Church, claim the Virgin Mary as our spiritual Mother. We belong to her household. We are members of her family. We share her spirit of faith, tenderness, and loving obedience.

We live in a new order ruled by a new principle. What is done *can* be undone. This basis of our new life in Christ goes by the name "forgiveness." We need not be bound by regret. We need not be overcome with remorse. Whatever wrongs we have done against our heavenly Father, He does not hold against us. When we come to Him, He forgives for the sake of Christ. Likewise, whatever grudges we might have against one another can be forgotten, because they can be forgiven.

So this Nativity fast is a good time to put aside all regret, resentment, bitterness, guilt, and lament in the power of the forgiveness of Christ and in the tenderheartedness of the Mother of God.

> *Because of the malady of disobedience,*
> *Eve received the curse within herself.*
> *But you, O Virgin Theotokos, have blossomed*
> *forth the blessing to all the world,*
> *by means of the One who sprang from your pregnancy.*
> *And therefore you do we magnify.*
> —MATINS FOR DECEMBER 19

# The Song of Faith
# Breaks the Silence

FR. BASIL ROSS ADEN

*So it was, on the eighth day, that they came to circumcise the child; and they would have called him by the name of his father, Zacharias. His mother answered and said, "No; he shall be called John." But they said to her, "There is no one among your relatives who is called by this name." So they made signs to his father—what he would have him called. And he asked for a writing tablet, and wrote, saying, "His name is John." So they all marveled. Immediately his mouth was opened and his tongue loosed, and he spoke, praising God. Then fear came on all who dwelt around them; and all these sayings were discussed throughout all the hill country of Judea. And all those who heard them kept them in their hearts, saying, "What kind of child will this be?" And the hand of the Lord was with him.*

—LUKE 1:59–66

Today we pray with the psalmist, "O Lord, You shall open my lips, and my mouth will declare Your praise" (Ps. 50/51:17). We were created for the praise of God, and the worship of the Holy Trinity is our destiny. Yet at times our voice of praise is muted and even silenced. At these times, we should pray that the Lord would so fill our hearts with faith that they overflow with songs of joy and thanksgiving.

Consider the father of St. John the Baptist, who lost and then regained his voice of praise. When the angel appeared to him in the temple, doubt tied Zacharias's tongue, and he was speechless until he proved faithful to the angel's message. When we reflect on Zacharias's experience, we might ask whether we also are spiritually tongue-tied. If so, what is the reason for our silence? Likewise, when it comes to giving glory to God, are we speechless? If that is the case, what is the remedy?

The psalmist says, "Bless the Lord, O my soul, and forget not all His rewards" (Ps. 102/103:2). This wisdom suggests that the reason we do not praise God is that we fail to acknowledge His constant benefits of goodness and mercy. Instead of looking to Him, we look to our own poor efforts to grab the good things God would freely give us.

Take Zacharias and Elizabeth. They had surely prayed fervently for a child. Yet when the angel announced the answer to their prayers, why did Zacharias doubt? Perhaps as the years went by, the priest had gradually given up on God. Long before he questioned the angel's message, he had concluded that the Lord would not or could not respond to his prayer.

In this way the song of joyful faith surrenders to the lamentation of gloomy doubt. Doubt, you see, is sullen and silent. It has nothing to say. It cannot praise God, for it denies the loving-kindness of God even while it discounts His power.

Praise, on the other hand, is the child of faith. When we put our trust in the power and goodness of God, we look to Him for

His mercy. And He does not disappoint us, for He exceeds our fondest desires and gives us more than we ask.

Doubt closed Zacharias's mouth to the praise of God even before the angel silenced his lips. But when the priest overcame his doubt and obeyed the angel, the Lord loosed his tongue. By the Holy Spirit, the priest who was unable to speak burst into majestic song.

From that song on, the jubilant sound of faith would break the silence of the world's doubt. As today's hymn proclaims, John would become the "voice of the Word." As that voice, the prophet announced even before his birth the coming of the Messiah, for when Mary, who was bearing the Christ Child, visited Elizabeth, John leapt in her womb. So as our hymn suggests, from his conception, the Prophet and Forerunner shouted the good news of the arrival of the Son of God.

Today's reading encourages us to pray that the Lord would loosen our tongues so that we might wholeheartedly praise the Holy Trinity. In this season of the Nativity fast, we hear the stories of the astonishing things the Lord has done for us. How can we remain in the darkness of doubt in the midst of the daylight of these works of love and mercy? If the Son of God can come down from heaven to be born of a Virgin; if the greatest prophet in history can be born of a barren woman; if a doubting priest can become the prime example of faith, obedience, and praise—what is impossible with God? And how can we not, in faith, "proclaim the praises of Him who called [us] out of darkness into His marvelous light" (1 Pet. 2:9)?

*When John was born, he broke the silence of Zacharias.*
*For it was no longer fitting that the father be unable to speak,*

*once he, the voice, had come forth.*
*When at first it was doubted, it tied the tongue;*
*now that it has shouted, it became him to release his father.*
*He announced to him the good news, and*
*he became the voice of the Word,*
*the Forerunner of the Light. And he intercedes for our souls.*
—VESPERS FOR THE NATIVITY OF
THE FORERUNNER, JUNE 24

# The Lord's "Advance Man"

### FR. BASIL ROSS ADEN

*"And you child, will be called the prophet of the Highest;*
*For you will go before the face of the Lord to prepare His*
*ways,*
*To give knowledge of salvation to His people*
*By the remission of their sins,*
*Through the tender mercy of our God,*
*With which the Dayspring from on high has visited us;*
*To give light to those who sit in the darkness and the shadow*
*of death,*
*To guide our feet into the way of peace."*

—LUKE 1:76–79

When the circus was coming to town, the first to arrive was the advance man. Living out of a suitcase, this traveling agent, promoter, and advertiser made all the preparations for the upcoming show. When he plastered the town with posters, he stirred up a frenzy of excitement about the upcoming extravaganza.

Today our hymn introduces John, the "voice of the Logos, the lantern of the Light, the morning star that preceded the Sun, the Forerunner in the desert." The Lord Jesus called this trumpet in the wilderness the greatest born of women (Luke

7:28) and more than a prophet (Matt. 11:9). About John, St. Peter of Damaskos asked, "What shall we call you, O Prophet, angel, apostle, martyr? Angel because you lived as though bodiless; apostle because you caught the nations in your net; martyr because you were beheaded for Christ's sake?"[11]

Why is John so praised? He was God's chosen advance man, sent to stir up the world's anticipation for the coming of the Savior. The prophet is the greatest person born because his calling was the greatest. He called the human race to the most important undertaking of all, the preparation for the saving work of the incarnate Son of God.

How do we answer John's urgent cry? Our hymn admonishes us to repent and purify ourselves. By the cleansing of sin, we should "prepare the way of the LORD; / Make His paths straight" (Luke 3:4).

This stirring call urges us to clear the path for Christ's coming. According to the Song of Zacharias, the Lord's visitation gives "knowledge of salvation . . . by the remission of their sins" (Luke 1:77). We may miss the significance of this thought. The Son of God will be born of the Virgin to confer the "knowledge of salvation." Yes, we seek salvation. But what is it? Is it deliverance from our earthly enemies, from whatever troubles us in this life? No, it is redemption from sin and its consequence of alienation from God. It is not relief from the hatred of our earthly enemies. It is redemption from our spiritual foes and freedom from captivity to the powers of sin, death, and the devil.

The billboards and signs of John, the advance man of the Messiah, call us to do some serious housekeeping in advance of the celebration of the Nativity. Accordingly, in this season of repentance, we put away the clutter of disobedience, take out the garbage of sin, and straighten up the house of our lives.

In the *Philokalia*, St. Gregory of Sinai notes what this housework should entail. It means obeying the commandments. But that requires a total realignment of the way we live and act so that everything we do lines up with the will of God.

However, St. Gregory goes on, "It is impossible to make straight the path of the commandments and to live rightly unless your heart is straight and upright."[12] Therefore, our purification must reach down deeply and directly into our hearts.

So then, in this Nativity fast, we are like the family who is expecting an honored guest. In joyful anticipation we set the table, decorate the house, clean the floors, cook the meals, and prepare the guest room of our hearts and lives. But we do not engage in the repentance of this season as if it were a list of onerous chores. Zacharias's exaltation at the birth of John sets the mood of celebration. Our preparation anticipates what is to come. Our housekeeping is the beginning of the party. Our fasting is the appetizer of our feasting.

The Lord's advance man has arrived. Today we rejoice in his call to prepare to celebrate the Birth of Jesus Christ, who comes as our Savior to give us the knowledge and experience of salvation by His redeeming grace.

> *The voice of the Logos, the lantern of the Light,*
> *the morning star that preceded the Sun,*
> *the Forerunner in the desert,*
> *crying out to all the peoples,*

*Repent and beforehand purify yourselves.*
*Behold, among us is the Christ, who out*
*of corruption redeems the world.*
—MATINS FOR JANUARY 1

# Mystery Beyond Reasoning

## FR. BASIL ROSS ADEN

*Now the birth of Jesus Christ was as follows: After His mother Mary was betrothed to Joseph, before they came together, she was found with child of the Holy Spirit. Then Joseph her husband, being a just man, and not wanting to make her a public example, was minded to put her away secretly.*

—MATTHEW 1:18–19

One of the most famous sculptures in the world is Auguste Rodin's *The Thinker*. It depicts a naked man perched on a rock, hunched over in deep thought. His fist is crammed into his lips, and his muscular body is tense with struggle; his mind is completely absorbed in contemplation.

First cast in 1904, the sculpture was part of the proposal for a museum that was never built. Rodin called the doors of the project *The Gates of Hell*, and *The Thinker* was to be seated above the depictions of the condemned in Dante's *Inferno*. Some interpreters speculate that the sculpture represents the fourteenth-century poet as he ponders the suffering of the souls in hell; others say he is contemplating the distress of human suffering.

Rodin's sculpture reminds us of one detail of the Orthodox icon of the Nativity. In that icon, we find Joseph off to the side, uninvolved in the Birth of the newborn Son of God. Hunched over, hand on his head, he is morose and troubled. An old man, the Tempter, leans on a staff before him, casting doubt in his mind.

The Scriptures leave it to us to imagine the feelings of the husband of Mary when she was found to be with child. But in today's hymn, Joseph laments that Mary has filled him with "dismay," shame, and sorrow. As a "just man," Joseph is torn between the divine Law's prescription of punishment for adultery and his compassion for his betrothed. After much soul-searching, he resolves his dilemma. He will judiciously put Mary away, divorcing his wife secretly to avoid making an example of her.

Joseph's decision goes as far as human reason can go. Like Rodin's *Thinker*, his thoughts are weighed down with the knowledge of human sorrow, suffering, and fallibility. Of all the characters in the story of the Lord's Incarnation, humanity can most identify with Joseph. He sits in the corner of God's work in the world and does not understand. With his human reasoning, he cannot comprehend the greatness of the mystery of God's will and ways. And the devil haunts him, sowing doubt and confusion in his mind. Joseph is a symbol of the truth that the ways of the Creator are unfathomable. Human reason cannot explain them, no matter how hard and long we ponder them.

We can be thankful that this is so, for if knowing God and His purposes were a matter of human understanding, then only the most intelligent thinkers could achieve it. But what God has hidden from the wise and educated, He has revealed to the humble and pure of heart. A young maiden, an older woman, a doubting priest, shepherds on the hills, foreigners from afar, and two aged worshippers in the temple are the greatest philosophers of the human race. They should be counted the wisest among us, for they believed in the promises of God fulfilled in the coming of the Lord, our Savior.

The children of God know that the mystery of the Incarnation of the Son of God is the key to the divine work of our redemption. So let Joseph join them in the understanding of faith. Let him hear in a dream that the baby born of the Virgin is the Son of God. Let him rise from sleep and do as the angel directed. Despising the shame, let him take Mary as his wife. And let the thinker climb down from the heights of his reasoning and begin the journey to Bethlehem, where he may find the joyful answer to his deep contemplation.

*Thus did Joseph speak to the Virgin,*
*"Mary, what is this I see in you?*
*I cannot understand it, and I am amazed,*
*and my mind is struck with dismay.*
*Therefore get out of my sight quickly.*
*Mary, what is this I see in you?*
*You have brought me reproach.*
*I cannot bear to be rebuked by the people.*
*When I received you from the priests in the*
*temple, you were an innocent girl,*
*consecrated to the Lord. So what is*
*this that I see in you now?"*
—GREAT HOURS FOR DECEMBER 24

# Faith & Conviction

FR. BASIL ROSS ADEN

*But while he thought about these things, behold, an angel of the Lord appeared to him in a dream, saying, "Joseph, son of David, do not be afraid to take to you Mary your wife, for that which is conceived in her is of the Holy Spirit. And she will bring forth a Son, and you shall call His name Jesus, for He will save His people from their sins."*

—MATTHEW 1:20–21

Among the saints whom we commemorate today is St. Crispina. The saint was arrested in AD 304 during the horrible Diocletian persecutions. Though imprisoned, humiliated, and threatened with torture and death, she refused to sacrifice to idols. In the blessed end of her earthly life, she was beheaded.

These stories are so typical that we might take their remarkable witness to the Faith for granted. But we might ask: What is the difference between these martyrs and ourselves? The answer is *conviction*. These heroes of the Faith held such a firm belief that they feared nothing except that they would betray their Lord.

Today in response to our Scripture passage, we cannot but wonder at the reversal of Joseph's intentions. When he learned of Mary's pregnancy, he was consumed with hurt, doubt, and perplexity. According to the customs of the day, Mary was his legal wife, though they were only betrothed. The only solution to his dilemma was to divorce her privately.

But now, because of a single dream, Joseph changed his mind overnight. Who would believe an angel who came in one's sleep to say that his betrothed would give birth to a Son conceived by the Holy Spirit? Who would obey a heavenly command to name the child Jesus, meaning "Savior"? Who would stake his future on the astonishing message that the Child would fulfill the prophecy to be Immanuel, God with Us? Joseph did.

In this Nativity fast, we might consider the strength of our belief. Are we like Joseph, who acted with firm faith in the Word of God? Or are we like the disciples, whose faith was weak, and who deserted the Lord when tested?

What is the difference between Joseph's fervent, active faith and weak, ineffective belief that does not produce the fruit of life-changing action? The hymn for the day asks Joseph how he came to change his mind about Mary, his betrothed. He answers that he is convinced that Mary is the Mother of God. His conviction impelled him to action. Joseph was so persuaded that he willingly did everything the Lord directed him to do.

Belief is opinion, whether or not it is correct. Belief is what we think to be true at the moment. It can be changed based on experience and evidence. Conviction, however, is firm faith, unmovable and unshakeable.

Conviction is like the yeast in the bread of our beliefs. It is the dynamic ingredient that makes faith fervent and active. Without it, our commitment to Christ is lukewarm—comfortable but fragile, assumed but not tested. No one risks their reputation and their life on halfhearted beliefs. No one who is wise builds their life on changeable conjectures. The salvation of our souls requires one thing: faith in the saving grace of God. But that faith must rest on the firm conviction that the Son of God has come to earth and that He has the power to redeem humanity from sin and death.

In this time of preparation for the Nativity of the Son of God, we confront the crucial matter of the fervor of our faith. Our example is Joseph, who responded to the test of his faithfulness with the confidence that Mary would bear the Son of God "in ways past understanding." The Scripture and hymn for today teach that this was not a casual conclusion. When Joseph verified the angelic message by a study of the Scriptures, unshakeable certainty replaced his wavering doubt.

The Lord has given us this time of prayer and fasting to firm up our faith. We praise God for His incredible mercy in the astonishing mystery of the Incarnation. And we honor Joseph for his part in the story of our salvation. Let us pray that the Holy Spirit would stir up our hearts with hope and joy but also with conviction. Then we will be prepared to act on the glorious glad tidings of this feast with the firm faith that leads to the active obedience of Joseph.

*Joseph, tell us, how is it that you bring to Bethlehem*
*the Maiden you received from the*
*temple, now great with child?*
*And he replies, "I have studied the prophetic books,*
*after receiving a revelation from an angel;*
*and I am convinced that Mary shall give birth to God,*

*in ways past understanding.*
*Magi will come from the East with*
*precious gifts to adore Him."*
*O Lord who took flesh for our sake, glory to You!*
—GREAT HOURS FOR THE EVE OF NATIVITY, DECEMBER 24

# A Living Icon of Charity

BRANDI WILLIS SCHREIBER

*The Spirit of the Lord is upon Me, because of which He anointed Me. He sent Me to proclaim good news to the poor, to heal the brokenhearted, to preach liberty to the captives and recovery of sight to the blind. . . . They shall be called genera-tions of righteousness, the planting of the Lord for glory.*

—ISAIAH 61:1, 3

Sometime around March 15, 270, a boy was born in Patara, in present-day Turkey. This little city, smelling of salt water and edged by the vibrant blues of water and sky, thrived as a maritime port. Today those blues are still backdropped by a bone-colored and rocky beach, but it was beyond this landscape, which now lies in ruins, and over its surrounding brushy green hills, in the neighboring city of Myra, that St. Nicholas lived most of his life.

Stories of Nicholas's early years abound. One of the most cherished describes his secret bequeathal of his inheritance to a poor family with three unmarried daughters. Without dowries to provide safety and protection, they had little hope of a secure future. Although these stories are worth reading for what they can teach us about a saint who intercedes in many ways, it's especially important to understand Nicholas's role as a bishop and how his saintly life teaches us to live out the gospel today.

The iconography of Nicholas contrasts greatly with the lackluster depictions of him as our modern "Santa." In some icons, he's clad in heavy garments patterned with bright, geometric crosses, but in every one of them, an *omophorion*, the distinct stole of a bishop, is draped around his shoulders. This stole boldly features large crosses, and Nicholas blesses the viewer with one hand while holding a Gospel book in the other.

These details—the eye-catching crosses, the ornate Gospel book with its bejeweled cover, the blessing hand—cannot escape the viewer's notice, for they clearly state that proclaiming the Gospel and the Incarnation of the Word to the world was and remains Nicholas's *true* profession.

Ordained as bishop of Myra somewhere around the year 300, Nicholas served a very public, and often fraught, role in which he daily and openly professed Christ and ministered to those around him—most notably the poor, sick, imprisoned, hungry, weary, and broken. This would have been no easy feat for him, having survived the brutal reign of Diocletian in his youth, and it is easy to understand how stories and legends endured from his time in Myra.

For his entire life, Nicholas heeded Christ's words. They moved through him in such a way that his only response was to act like Him. To serve and give and be like Him. Through Nicholas's generosity, devotion, and work, he lived the prophecy in Isaiah to "proclaim good news . . . heal . . . [and] preach." It is also through this legacy that he indeed did the work as a "planting of the Lord for glory," so much so that his inspiring life continues to reach us today.

When we stand before an icon of St. Nicholas, either in the soft light of our homes or in the illuminated vibrancy of our churches, we must remember that he still proclaims the Good News of the Incarnation. Nicholas still wears the cross. He still blesses us and holds the Word before us in his hand.

In return, we must ask ourselves how we outwardly manifest the same things. In what way today, for example, might we publicly wear the cross of Christ and proclaim the Good News to someone who needs to hear it? What small and secret act of charity can we do? How can we ease a sorrowful heart or provide for the spiritual or physical needs of someone on the fringe of our daily life, outside our comfortable circles and routines?

Nicholas, in all his years of guiding and inspiring souls, is here to help us. We can imitate that young boy standing on the edge of an ancient coast and wondering what to do with the inheritance he'd been given. We can pray to him and ask him for his guidance. We can share his example with our children, our families, and our communities, just as he did.

Saint Nicholas, pray for us. May we come to model all the best virtues you exhibit.

*The truth of things revealed you to*
*your flock as a rule of faith,*
*a model of meekness and teacher of abstinence;*
*wherefore, you have attained the heights through*
*humility and riches through poverty.*
*O Hierarch Nicholas our father, entreat*
*Christ God that our souls be saved.*
—VESPERS FOR ST. NICHOLAS OF MYRA, DECEMBER 6

# God with Us

### BRANDI WILLIS SCHREIBER

*So all this was done that it might be fulfilled which was spoken by the Lord through the prophet, saying: "Behold, the virgin shall be with child, and bear a Son, and they shall call His name Immanuel," which is translated, "God with us." Then Joseph, being aroused from sleep, did as the angel of the Lord commanded him and took to him his wife, and did not know her till she had brought forth her firstborn Son. And he called His name Jesus.*

—MATTHEW 1:22–25

It's a powerful claim: God is with us. We see transcribed in the icon of the Nativity, in which the light of heaven points to a newborn Child next to His mother, all angels and earth focused on the physical reality God has assumed—His presence in our midst.

Yet how often we wonder if He is *really* with us, all the time. In the same icon, a doubtful St. Joseph is often depicted in a lower corner, distant from the jubilant scene. His head hangs in his hands while the evil one whispers into his ear to "put [Mary] away secretly" (Matt. 1:19).

God seems to be with us when things are going well, we understand what is happening, and we can take a snapshot of our pretty and well-ordered lives.

But it's in the times when we are forsaken and unsure—when we've lost a job or a child, endured the death of our dreams, or become so broken with sin we're unrecognizable, even to ourselves—that we really question if God is *truly* with us.

In the Healing Prayer of St. Ambrose of Milan (whom we also celebrate today), the saint addresses this very question by highlighting that separation from God is not dependent on external circumstances—what we've achieved and understand—but on what is within us. "For what shall separate me," he asks, quoting from St. Paul in Romans 8, "from the love of God, which is in Thee? Shall tribulation, or distress, or famine?" He then addresses the reader with the excitement of a revelation that simply must be shared: "Hear me, you earthly men, who in your sins bring forth drunken thoughts: I have found a Physician, . . . He alone who knows what is hidden can take away the grief of my heart, the fear of my soul: Jesus Christ."

Saint Ambrose understood that our sin causes separation from God and the distortion (drunken thoughts) through which we view our lives. He also provides some of the earliest words describing the Church as a hospital for the soul and Christ as its key Physician. Christ is the Healer who not only understands the fear and sickness of our circumstances but is the only One who can restore us. He heals us because He knows what it is to suffer alongside us. Through the Incarnation, He entered into everything we experience in our lives—our physical nature with its temptations, limitations, and emotional turmoil—so that

He might restore us. There is nowhere God is not, including our pain.

In Psalm 138/139, the psalmist discusses the God who is everywhere present and filling all things:

Where could I go from Your Spirit,
Or flee from Your face?
If I should ascend into heaven, You would be there;
If I should descend into Hades, You would be there;
If I should take up my wings at dawn
And pitch camp at the furthest part of the sea,
Even there Your hand would lead me. . . .
I awakened, and I am still with You. (vv. 7–10, 18)

The psalmist knew God would be there when he awakened. And He was, just as He was with Joseph, full of uncertainty over the strange situation in which he found himself. God likewise remains with us.

We will no doubt encounter seasons when we may doubt God's presence in our lives. The Church, however, provides thousands of resources to help us remember His promise to remain in our midst.

We can emulate St. Joseph's faithful obedience and do what God asks of us, although we may question His purpose. We can read the Healing Prayer of St. Ambrose of Milan and remind ourselves that our "drunken thoughts" are not the truth and that a Physician is waiting to heal us, if we will just let Him. We can also look closely at the icon of the Nativity and notice that the newborn Christ is shrouded not in the swaddling clothes of a baby, but in the burial wrappings of death: a foreshadowing of what is to come and a reminder that God is with us unto death and beyond.

We praise You, Emmanuel! God is with us!

*Never has anyone been so poor as our God,*
*or so rich as Adam, recreated in godliness,*
*the Virgin cried out as she held Him in her arms*
*Emmanuel, our God and Creator,*
*who had clothed Himself with flesh from her.*
*Let us cry to Him:*
*Blessed are You, our newborn God: glory to You!*
—MATINS FOR DECEMBER 28

# Turning Eastward

BRANDI WILLIS SCHREIBER

*Then He brought me back to the outer gate of the sanctuary that faces toward the east, but it was shut. So the Lord said to me, "This gate shall be shut. It shall not be opened, and no man shall pass through it, because the Lord God of Israel will enter by it; therefore, it shall be shut. As for the prince, he will sit in it to eat bread before the Lord. He will go in by way of the gate chamber and go out the same way."*

—EZEKIEL 44:1–3

This morning, the eastern sky burns rose gold. A storm rolled in overnight, and its remnants—clouds pinched thin and low over the treetops—refract the first light of day into incandescent colors. As the sun rises behind the clouds, the hues intensify from golden pink to tangerine before the light breaks into fingers of shimmering yellow. It is a scene worthy of a painting, if an artist could capture it quickly enough. As soon as it begins, however, it is over. The sun crests; the clouds dissipate. All that is left is the crystal blue of morning.

We Orthodox Christians are always drawn to the east. East is our original home, where we first met our Father in a garden. It is the direction toward which Moses faced his tent and Solomon oriented the Lord's gate on his temple; it is the direction where Christ ascended and from where He will return. "For as lightning comes from the east," He tells His disciples in Matthew 24:27, "so also will the coming of the Son of Man be."

East is the orientation of our worship. We stand facing east in our churches, venerate icons on eastern walls, slowly move eastward as we approach the chalice. We look, sing, and pray toward the east, longing for relationship with Christ and union with our good God. "The east is assigned to him for worship," St. John of Damascus writes, "for everything beautiful should be assigned to God, from whom every good thing derives its goodness."[13] Christ Himself is the East, "the Orient from on High" (Luke 1:78, Douay-Rheims Bible).

In the hymns and prayers of the Church, Mary is often referred to as "the Gate facing the East" or "the Eastern Gate." Through her virtuousness and willing participation, she became the physical doorway—the means—for Christ to come down to participate in humanity with us through the Incarnation. When we are lost and don't know which way to turn, we can remember that the Theotokos models how to pursue God and seek ever to be closer to Him. She reminds us we can turn eastward.

In Ezekiel 44, the prophet is shown the doors of the outer gate of the sanctuary, a gate that faces east. "This gate shall be shut," he is told, "and no man shall pass through it." Only the Lord, the God of Israel, the Glory of God Himself—Christ—will cross over its threshold, and once that happens, the gate is sealed and shut forever.

This is a powerful prefiguring of the Incarnation through Mary, who is also called "the Temple of the Lord" and "the Gate of Heaven." This prophecy reveals she is not just the Virgin Mary, but the *Ever*-Virgin Mary. She is the holy temple of God

Most High and His very dwelling place. The Church teaches us that she conceived the Christ Child in virginity through the Holy Spirit, gave birth to Him without losing her virginity, and remained a virgin the rest of her life. Her ever-virginity remains an unbroken tradition of the Church, defended for two thousand years and referenced in almost all her services.

In her ever-virginity, of course, we encounter a miracle, something inexplicable. But as St. Ambrose of Milan wisely noted, "A virgin giving birth is the sign of a divine mystery, not a human one."[14] This divine mystery is a gift to contemplate, just like the indescribable brilliance of this morning's sky and all the ways God shares His majesty and works His wonders. As we contemplate the mystery of these things and the great love through which God makes this reality possible to us, let's take a moment to stop.

Turn eastward, wherever we are. Say a brief prayer. Note what we see. Remember that God provides every blessing, preserves everything good.

And thank Him for it all.

*Sprung from the stem of Jesse, Holy Virgin,*
*you have passed beyond the boundaries of human nature,*
*for you have borne the pre-eternal Word of the Father*
*according to His good pleasure; by a strange self-emptying,*
*He passed through your womb, yet kept it sealed.*
—MATINS FOR THE NATIVITY OF CHRIST, DECEMBER 25

# Bearing Fruit in God's Time

BRANDI WILLIS SCHREIBER

*And, behold, an angel of the Lord stood by, saying: Anna,
Anna, the Lord has heard your prayer, and you shall conceive,
and shall bring forth; and your seed shall be spoken of in all the
world. And Anna said: As the Lord my God lives, if I bear
either male or female, I will bring it as a gift to the Lord my
God; and it shall minister to Him in holy things all the days
of its life.*

—PROTOEVANGELION OF JAMES 4

O utside the window, a pecan tree grows against an old shed.
Half the view is its astonishing height; the other half is
the neighbor's cluster of trees, a striking blue sky, sometimes a
red-tailed hawk disappearing into both.

The tree's branches drift today as if they are sailing on an
ocean and not moving within a hot West Texas wind. It must
have been an accident, this tree, sprouted from a nut a squirrel
buried and forgot decades ago. Or perhaps it was thoughtlessly
planted, for it creaks too closely against the shed's shingles. For
years after we moved into this house, the tree did nothing more
than provide a half-shade in summer and release massive fans of

leaves that had to be raked out of the rosemary in autumn. A lot of work for no harvest.

Until last year, when it finally fruited and rained down pecans.

They hit the patio like hail, delighting the dog, the squirrels, the baby, who learned to retrieve them with his dimpled hands. They rolled into flower beds, thumped against cars in the driveway. Pecans for weeks. For everyone. Given as gifts, bagged in the freezer, still waiting in bowls this morning to be cracked and mixed into oatmeal and cakes.

The tree's season of fruitfulness had come, unannounced, unanticipated. Likewise, the teaching of the Church about the parents of Mary, Ss. Joachim and Anna—the grandparents of Christ—is filled with the beautiful echoes of a God who brings forth blessed fruit in His own perfect and incontestable time.

Tradition tells us that Joachim and Anna were steadfast and faithful to the Lord, giving more than the required tithe to the temple and to the poor. However, Anna was barren, longing for a child well into old age. In ancient Jewish society, barrenness was seen as a curse or disgrace. It did not matter that Joachim and Anna were faithful and generous beyond measure, serving as examples of how to love God. Having no children was grievous.

The Protoevangelion of James, which preserves this tradition, records Anna's lamentations as she compares herself to sparrows, waters, the earth—all fruitful except for her. Beneath a laurel tree, she pleads with God: "O God of our fathers, bless me and hear my prayer, as You blessed the womb of Sarah and gave her a son" (Prot. Jas. 2).

God hears Anna's prayer and grants her motherhood with a daughter—a miracle for a woman her age. In return, Anna promises to bring Mary to the temple to serve God "as a gift," which she and Joachim did when Mary was about three years old (Prot. Jas. 7). Saint Anna gave back to God all that He gave her, just as she had given to those around her.

The preparation for the coming of Christ, therefore, has its noble roots not just in Mary but in her parents as well, showing us how extensive God's providence really is. Although Joachim and Anna fell asleep in the Lord before Mary reached adolescence, leaving her an orphan, they laid the foundation—through their faithfulness, obedience, and love—for Mary's astounding devotion to God and her own preparation to become the Mother of Christ.

Anna couldn't possibly have imagined the woman Mary would become or the role she would play in the salvation of the world through the birth of *her* Child.

At any time in her advanced years, Anna could have relinquished her request to God to become a mother. But she didn't. She prayed for the impossible—pregnancy after nearly fifty years of barren, married life—knowing that God could deliver what seemed impossible. He had done it before, after all.

The mystery of God's provision is the same with this pecan tree, whose ripening fruit is hidden in the shadows of its leaves. It is the same with us when we continue to pray, to ask, to press on with our God, who responds to our requests according to His will.

He will rain down His blessings when it is time. And we will gather drifts of them.

*The barren woman who, in manner past hope,*
*bears as fruit her who will give birth to God in the flesh*
*is made radiant with joy and dances,*
*rejoicing and crying aloud:*
*"Let all the tribes of Israel rejoice with me!*
*For lo! I have conceived in my womb*
*and put away the disgrace of barrenness:*
*for thus has the Creator been well pleased, and,*
*hearkening to my prayer in those things which I have desired,*
*He has healed the pain of my heart."*
—VESPERS FOR THE POST-FEAST OF THE
NATIVITY OF THE THEOTOKOS, DECEMBER 9

# A Faith That Is Seen and Heard

### BRANDI WILLIS SCHREIBER

*And it came to pass in those days that a decree went out from Caesar Augustus that all the world should be registered. This census first took place while Quirinius was governing Syria. So all went to be registered, everyone to his own city. Joseph also went up from Galilee, out of the city of Nazareth, into Judea, to the city of David, which is called Bethlehem, because he was of the house and lineage of David, to be registered with Mary, his betrothed wife, who was with child.*

—LUKE 2:1–5

The blue-black of early morning, a few hours before sunrise, is my favorite time to walk. Cloistered in the quiet of my sleeping neighborhood, I experience a magic hour where all things hidden in shadow during the day—russet foxes with black-tipped tails, possums the hue of fog—are awake and busy between houses.

At these times, my walk is my own. I'm unseen, uninterrupted by others. No demands are placed on me; I am selfishly alone, secret. Only when I encounter another early jogger, or the sweet lady who retrieves her newspaper with her corgi, do I feel exposed. Suddenly, I am seen, and being seen reminds me that when my walk is over, I must return to the world and the day's uncertainties.

We think sometimes there is safety in anonymity, in living unnoticed. It is comfortable and convenient, but not always the way God asks us to live.

Saint Joseph no doubt struggled with the attention he received when he became Mary's husband. A fourteenth-century icon in the Kariye Djami (the Church of the Holy Savior, now a mosque, in present-day Istanbul) hints at this. In faded tones of blues, golds, and mossy green, an anxious Joseph escorts a small and heavily dressed Mary, her wide eyes transfixed on her husband, through the town to his house. The hems of his garments flutter around his feet with his pace as he casts an uncertain look behind him at his new wife. "This way," his hands seem to gesture ahead of him. "Quickly, before anyone sees us!"

He is concerned, having been saddled with the enormous and visible responsibility of this young maiden. He's already lived a full life, been married and widowed with children of his own. Whatever will people think when they see him married to this girl?

Now he must care for a young and very pregnant wife, and, as Luke's Gospel tells us, also register his entire household with the authorities. We cannot forget that the Jews of the time lived under the often brutal rule of the Romans. The lands were no longer theirs, and these were not their kings, yet foreign rulers demanded they pay taxes—the purpose of the census. To be registered was to be visible to a regime whose intentions were not always benevolent toward the people they governed. What might happen to Joseph? To his income? To the very young maiden of God and her unborn Child, now in his care?

Any trepidation Joseph felt would be understandable.

Yet he acted in humble obedience, despite fear, worry, and—scariest of all—the unknown. He loaded up his pregnant wife to make the long journey from Nazareth to Bethlehem, his hometown, where he was required to register. By God's providence, Bethlehem was also the town where the Scriptures promised the Messiah would be born. Joseph was asked to sacrifice his comfort, reputation, and perhaps even his life for the redemption of the entire world.

We can be comforted, therefore, knowing God uses everything to accomplish His will, including earthly rulers. Our role is to remain humbly obedient. And trust Him.

Years later, Christ tells the chief priests and scribes seeking to ensnare Him over the issue of paying taxes that we must "render therefore to Caesar the things that are Caesar's, and to God the things that are God's" (Luke 20:25). Christ didn't enter the world to live quietly or to work comfortably from the shadows. He was registered right along with His parents and the rest of the fallen world so that we might be registered with Him in Paradise. During the remainder of His earthly life until His death and triumphant Resurrection, He was seen and heard. He worked in the world, but He remained of God.

We can do this, too.

When we operate in faith and publicly love Him, serve Him, and help others, we can live with the confidence that God will see us and take care of us, too, despite whatever is happening in the world. We can be known.

We can walk into a new day's sunrise and face anything waiting for us there.

*You have appeared on earth, living with mortal men;*
*obeying the decree of Caesar, You were*
*enrolled with Your servants.*
*You came as man; You did not abandon us,*
*remaining the true and changeless God, although incarnate.*
*Glory to your dispensation!*
*Worship, praise, dominion, and majesty,*
*now and ever and unto ages of ages. Amen!*
—MATINS FOR DECEMBER 23

# An Arduous Journey to Glory

BRANDI WILLIS SCHREIBER

*I will not fear by day,*
*But I will hope in You.*
*I will praise God with my words all day long;*
*In God I hope; I will not be afraid; what will flesh do to me?*
—PSALM 55/56:4–5

For many women, a moment arrives in pregnancy in which the body shifts from pleasant awareness of growing life to discomfort. Suddenly everything hurts, and one wonders how the body can get any heavier, fuller, more stretched when *the baby isn't even here yet.*

These sensations herald the need for quiet rest and preparation. For softness and nourishment. For peace and familiarity to strengthen the mother for what's to come.

But pregnancy was a different experience for the Theotokos. About one week before the Christ Child's arrival, Mary wasn't enveloped in the warm fires of home. Instead, she was draped in the heavy cloaks of winter. She balanced on the back of a donkey, leaning into its rough neck for support. She walked across dirt and stone. The home she knew had long since faded behind her, and she strained to see the City of David somewhere, anywhere, on the horizon.

She was on her way to Bethlehem (Luke 2:4–5).

By foot, from Nazareth to Bethlehem is an arduous ninety-mile journey of constant ascents and descents. Traveling through hills, mountains punctuated by steep escarpments, and rocky, dusty plains, Mary and Joseph would have been hounded by anxiety over missteps and injury—perhaps even death.

Slow and exhausting days were followed by nights wrapped in darkness and freezing temperatures. Food would have been meager; water would have been rationed. Threats of inclement weather, wild beasts, and robbers—or worse—along their path remained ever present.

Complicating all of this, of course, was Mary's state: heavy with child, full to the point of overflowing, stretched in containment of all the heavens. The Christ Child would come at any moment, but not until the ochre outline of Bethlehem appeared.

Until then, she must endure.

It is almost impossible to imagine Mary on such a long and arduous journey while pregnant. Yet tradition teaches us she maintained her hope and joy, anticipating the fulfillment of Archangel Gabriel's words to her: "You *will* conceive in your womb and bring forth a Son, and *shall* call His name JESUS" (Luke 1:31, emphasis mine). Within this proclamation lingers a beautiful anticipation.

Bethlehem, surrounded by its windswept hills and caves of gray limestone, anticipated the Birth of the Messiah, too. As the prophecy of Micah, written seven hundred years prior, reminds us, the little town that was "fewest in number among the thousands of Judah" would yield "the One to be ruler of Israel. His goings forth were from the beginning, even from everlasting"

(Mic. 5:1). The One who would change the world forevermore would arrive at its doorstep that blessed night, but Bethlehem's preparation would not include the waiting fires and hospitality of a guesthouse.

Instead, a humble cave would open, and beasts and shepherds would welcome the Savior.

We recall this anticipation even today during the service of the Proskomedia, which takes place before the Divine Liturgy, when the priest says, "Make ready, O Bethlehem; for Eden has been opened to all. Prepare yourself . . . for the tree of life has blossomed from the Virgin in the cave. . . . Christ is born, to raise up the image which before was fallen."

These beautiful words, recited in some traditions in front of the icon of the Nativity, connect us to the holy journey Mary endured. They remind us that we, too, must *prepare* before we can see Christ. We must *endure* the world—and ourselves. We must *labor* before we partake of Him and the Kingdom He brings.

In a way, all of life, including our movement to the Eucharist, is a slow and sometimes arduous journey into Bethlehem. Life makes us suffering travelers—aching, weary, full to the point of breaking—but we need not endure it in fear. Like Mary, we can be reminded of the joyous destination that awaits us. "Put away all your fears," the hymn from Great Hours of Nativity Eve tells us below, "and understand the extraordinary wonder. . . . You will see Him born of me."

The journey *will* end. And Glory awaits.

*O Virgin Mary, when Joseph was racked*
*with sadness, on the way to Bethlehem,*
*you said to him, "Why are you miserable*
*and troubled, seeing me pregnant?*
*Are you completely ignorant of the*
*tremendous mystery unfolding in me?*
*Well then, put away all your fears, and*
*understand the extraordinary wonder.*
*God, in His mercy, has come down to earth,*
*and He is now in my womb, and He has taken flesh.*
*You will see Him born of me, as He will;*
*and you will be filled with joy;*
*and you will worship Him as your Creator,*
*the One whom angels unceasingly extol and glorify,*
*as they do the Father and the Holy Spirit."*

—GREAT HOURS FOR THE EVE OF NATIVITY, DECEMBER 24

# Emulating the Good Shepherd

### BRANDI WILLIS SCHREIBER

*I am the good shepherd; and I know My sheep, and am known by My own. As the Father knows Me, even so I know the Father; and I lay down my life for the sheep. And other sheep I have which are not of this fold; them also I must bring, and they will hear My voice; and there will be one flock and one shepherd.*

—JOHN 10:14–16

Near the end of the third century, a humble shepherd was born on a little gold and green island in the eastern Mediterranean Sea.

His parents, tradition teaches, were poor and uneducated. Unable to read, he memorized the Bible by hearing it read in church. As he passed his boyhood days driving herds up and down the fertile grazing grounds of his homeland, he grew in piety and love for God, teaching those he met about the One who came down to redeem humanity.

In time, his island's love for him grew so much that he was ordained a priest and then elected bishop. Although his status grew, he continued to preach and serve with staggering humility. His clothing remained unembellished, his manner of speech unpretentious—perhaps even a bit coarse, according to some accounts. When he attended the first Council of Nicaea in 325, he shocked the assembly with his impoverished appearance, but more so with his defense of the Orthodox Faith. At one point, he used a broken piece of pottery to explain the concept of the Holy Trinity: fire, earth, and water in one shard. He is still depicted in his icon holding that potsherd and wearing a shepherd's hat.

Saint Spyridon the Wonderworker is one of the most beloved saints of Cyprus and the entire Orthodox Church. Although he rose to the rank of bishop and performed many healing miracles and other wonders, he stayed a "preacher of the people." His approach was simple: he spoke about the gospel in terms the common people could understand, and he worked a common job, too, keeping his own animals while he ministered to his spiritual flock until his repose, somewhere around 348.

Shepherding is exhausting, unglamorous work. A shepherd drives his herds through dirt and dung to nourishment and water. He must protect his animals from predators and disease, assist with births, nurse weak babies. Even as sheep and goats come to know their master, they can be stubborn and unpredictable creatures, wandering from the group's safety. Rare is the shepherd—especially in ancient times—who would leave an entire flock vulnerable to retrieve a straggler.

When Christ told the unbelieving Jews in John 10:11–15 that He knew His sheep and would lay down His life for them, they were confused by His saying. A shepherd who would die for his sheep? What nonsense!

Christ never compares Himself to the ruler of an empire or a great commander of armies. Rather, He likens Himself to the homeliest of vocations to help his audience—including us—truly understand our value and the lengths to which He will go to rescue us and reunite us to Him.

As the Good Shepherd, Christ cares for us despite our baseness, guides us to the "green pastures" of His rest and replenishment (Ps. 22/23:2), and surrenders everything—even His life—to find us when we stray (Matt. 18:12–14). How astonishing it is to know we are loved *that much* and can worship a God who so willingly embodies such a role.

Indeed, from the very night of His Birth—long before the Good Shepherd would be led away to His own slaughter—He lovingly and profoundly reveals His love for all, no matter their status or station.

For there were other poor shepherds among the hills and caves of Bethlehem that glorious night, men guarding their flocks by the stars. Angels peeled back the black sky and sang His arrival especially to them, tired and dirty as they were from their hard work, their sheep's rough bodies huddling near for warmth. These were the first to hear the news of the Christ Child's Birth.

Saint Spyridon emulated the Good Shepherd all his life. Today, let us ask ourselves how we can be like him. How can we humbly serve all of God's creation? And like those poor shepherds standing astonished in the dust, how can we hold and share their same wonder? And in this Nativity season, how can we more fully praise the Good Shepherd, who still leaves everything behind to find each and every one of us?

No matter where we may wander.

*Taking you from a flock as He had David,*
*the Creator appointed you, Spyridon,*
*as a most eminent shepherd of the rational flock,*
*shining forth in simplicity and meekness,*
*and adorned with guilelessness, O venerable pastor.*

—MATINS FOR ST. SPYRIDON, DECEMBER 12

# Fallow Time

ELISSA BJELETICH DAVIS

*So it was, that while they were there, the days were completed for her to be delivered. And she brought forth her firstborn Son, and wrapped Him in swaddling cloths, and laid Him in a manger, because there was no room for them in the inn.*

—LUKE 2:6–7

How long did Israel wait? For how many years did Israel anticipate the coming King?

So many prophets came and went throughout those long years, and God's people waited. They made their way through the wilderness and through history, always with the promise that God would send the Messiah, who would lead Israel to glory. Surely it seemed at times that their Savior would never come.

Perhaps we know how that feels, as we await our Lord's Second Coming. Sometimes it feels close, and yet, after almost two thousand years, He has still not come. We hold fast to our faith that He will rise like the sun in the East, coming again in glory to judge the living and the dead.

We wait.

Israel held onto that faith, and then, thousands of years after Abraham was told that his own seed would bring salvation to all the tribes of the earth, it finally happened: "So it was . . . the days were completed."

In God's time, in the fullness of time, Mary brought forth the Son. Our uncontainable God burst into the world, incarnate, and everything changed.

God always acts at the right moment, and somehow, we never know when that moment will be. We learn to wait.

Farmers have long rotated their crops, cultivating different plants at various times, to protect their fertile soil from depletion. These practices call for a periodic fallow time, when the land is plowed and harrowed but left unsown. As the field sits, resting and empty, it looks like nothing is happening. But in truth, in that quiet period of rest, millions of microscopic organisms are at work transforming the soil, making it rich and ready.

During this Nativity fast, we count the days. We learn to wait. We avoid the burnout of overproduction by embracing the liturgical calendar, allowing for seasons of peace and reflection. Perhaps a fast is our heart's fallow time: we appear quieter and less active than usual, but under the surface, we are regenerating and growing more fertile. Our hearts are transformed in this stillness that we might bear fruit when we emerge.

We are learning patience. We are learning to sit in the stillness, to pray and to listen for God. And we are preparing ourselves, that Christ's seeds might take root in the fertile soil of our hearts. We hope to be ready to receive Him at the Feast of His Nativity.

Israel waited for so many generations for the King of kings to arrive, and when, in the fullness of time, our Lord was finally born in Bethlehem, the city had not prepared a place for Him. There was no room in the inn. They were not quite ready to receive Him.

Instead, the earth presented a cave: creation made room to receive its Creator. The earth knew its Maker, and the animals adored the baby beside them. The star shone brightly, announcing His presence. All of creation praises Him forever.

We are part of His wondrous creation, and we too must open up the caves of our hearts. We must make room for the coming of the Lord.

This fast is the fallow time. We make time for prayer and study; we allow the words of the Scriptures and the saints to go to work in our hearts, regenerating and transforming the soil. Let us be ready, for this time too will pass, and He will come to us.

The God before all the ages arrives right on time, as always. All time belongs to God, and only God recognizes the fullness of time: only He can choose the acceptable time.

*Today, the Virgin bears Him who is transcendent,*
*and the earth presents the cave to Him who is beyond reach.*
*Angels, along with shepherds, glorify Him.*
*The Magi make their way to Him by a star.*
*For a new child has been born for us, the God before all ages.*
—KONTAKION OF HOLY NATIVITY, DECEMBER 24

# Unveiled Faces

ELISSA BJELETICH DAVIS

*And the Word became flesh and dwelt among us, and we beheld His glory, the glory as of the only begotten of the Father, full of grace and truth.*

—JOHN 1:14

The Gospel of St. John opens with such poetic theology: "In the beginning was the Word, and the Word was with God, and the Word was God" (1:1). In the beginning, before all ages, in the vast, dark chaos, was the Word, and He created all things out of nothing. He always was, and He always will be.

"The Word became flesh and dwelt among us, and we beheld His glory" (v. 14).

Before the Word became flesh, we could not behold His glory. We remember Isaiah, who saw God on His throne, surrounded by hosts of angels, and cried, "Woe is me, because I am pierced to the heart, for being a man and having unclean lips, I dwell in the midst of a people with unclean lips; for I saw the King, the Lord of hosts, with my eyes!" (Is. 6:5).

In his second letter to the Corinthians, St. Paul reminds us that before the Word took flesh, in the days of the Old Testament, it was necessary for Moses to "put a veil over his face so that the children of Israel could not look steadily at the end of what was passing away" (2 Cor. 3:13)—that is, at the glorified skin of his face, still resplendent after coming down from the mountain, having spoken with God. Even in this indirect way, in the face of Moses, beholding the glory of God was too much. *We have unclean lips, and we dwell in the midst of a people with unclean lips. We cannot look upon it.*

But now, the Word has taken flesh and dwelt among us. The incomprehensible and uncontainable God has done the unthinkable: He has condescended to enter into His Creation. God is glorious on His throne, surrounded by hosts of angels, but He is also glorious wrapped in swaddling clothes, asleep in a humble manger, tiny and perfect and incomprehensible.

Fully God and fully man, He dwells among us, and everything is transformed. Now we behold His glory. Saint Paul continues, "But we all, with unveiled face, beholding as in a mirror the glory of the Lord, are being transformed into the same image from glory to glory, just as by the Spirit of the Lord" (2 Cor. 3:18). What a thing to say: we see, *as in a mirror,* the glory of God. We look at ourselves, and we see something of God, the image of God into which He is transforming us, *from glory to glory.* We are called to something entirely new, both to behold His glory and to participate in it.

Cleansed in baptism and sealed with the Holy Spirit, nourished in Holy Communion with our Lord, we are now given a path that leads from glory to glory. Washed clean of our sins again and again, by faithfully living the sacramental life of the Church, by prayer and fasting and almsgiving, our unclean lips are slowly washed, our hearts are slowly purified and softened.

In clean baptismal garments, we may enter into the banquet and meet our Lord, face to face.

This is the great gift of our Lord, the amazing fruit of His Incarnation. We are given a path not just to be with Him, but to become more like Him—to look in the mirror and behold His glory.

In those moments when our Nativity fast feels dry or tiresome, let's remind ourselves that this is no empty obligation. This is our natural response to our Lord's great mercy; we show our gratitude and love by responding to Christ's great generosity with our own. Let us fast generously and joyfully, for we are walking every day the path that brings us out from the darkness of sin, the path that embraces Christ's profound gift. We move from glory to glory, ever more entwined with our Lord.

*He is come made flesh, Christ our God,*
*whom from the womb before the morning star*
*does God the Father beget.*
*He who rides upon the immaculate host of the heavenly minds*
*now is laid in a manger of irrationals.*
*He is wrapped in tattered swaddling clothes,*
*but He looses transgressions' entangling bonds.*
—MATINS FOR NATIVITY, DECEMBER 25

# The Unexpected Ones

### ELISSA BJELETICH DAVIS

*Now there were in the same country shepherds living out in the fields, keeping watch over their flock by night. And behold, an angel of the Lord stood before them, and the glory of the Lord shone around them, and they were greatly afraid. Then the angel said to them, "Do not be afraid, for behold, I bring you good tidings of great joy which will be to all people. For there is born to you this day in the city of David a Savior, who is Christ the Lord. And this will be the sign to you: You will find a Babe wrapped in swaddling cloths, lying in a manger." And suddenly there was with the angel a multitude of the heavenly host praising God and saying:*

*"Glory to God in the highest,*
*And on earth peace, goodwill toward men!"*

—LUKE 2:8–14

How tranquil the scene, as shepherds keep watch over their flocks at night. We can imagine the cool silence of the evening, the peace of the sleeping lambs, the whisper of the breeze as it stirs the nearby trees. How peaceful, how quiet.

The shepherds around Bethlehem lived a quiet life, a decidedly unglamorous life. Their days were spent alone, with only the bleating of sheep for conversation. Long quiet walks out into the same hills day after day, allowing the sheep to graze; the hottest part of the afternoon spent dozing under a bit of shade. The shepherd's life moved at a terribly slow pace, with little entertainment or diversion. Their silent nights were likely not much quieter than their long, wearying days.

Meanwhile, back in the village, life bustled. Friends greeted one another in the streets, business was transacted, and people chattered. In the cool morning hours, the ladies gathered to fill their jugs at the well and to exchange the latest news and gossip. Armed with water to nourish their households, they returned to their kitchens, among the first to know the news.

How long would it take for that news, the day's titillating gossip, to reach the ears of the shepherds? Their ears were trained to hear the footfalls of a predator, to monitor the murmurs of the flock, but they did not often keep up with current events. Shepherds were always out of the loop.

And yet, on this night, our God would challenge all our assumptions: the King of kings would be born in a cave rather than a palace, surrounded by livestock instead of servants. This stunning news would come first not to those at the center of a culture, but to the most isolated of its people. For behold, an angel of the Lord stood there, before these unlikely, disconnected shepherds, and the glory of the Lord shone around them, and they were greatly afraid.

What a tremendous contrast: the bright light of this glorious angel in the midst of the dark desert night. The humble, quiet shepherds stand before the towering, gleaming angel and are the first to receive news meant for all humanity: "Do not be afraid, for behold, I bring you good tidings of great joy which will be to all people. For there is born to you this day in the city of David a Savior, who is Christ the Lord. And this *will be* the sign to you: You will find a Babe wrapped in swaddling cloths, lying in a manger."

This, the greatest news of all time, comes with instructions to find the Lord Himself in a manger in Bethlehem. The divine, profound assignment, their holy commission, is given to the humble shepherds, and the night erupts in light and song: "Glory to God in the highest, / and on earth peace, goodwill toward men!" The shepherds must now depart: they must go and see.

On the morning of our Lord's Resurrection, the news would reach the myrrhbearing women first—not the men, not the apostles, but the humble women who showed up at dawn to do the hard work of preparing and honoring the body. Angels would appear before them in shining garments and ask, "Why do you seek the living among the dead? He is not here, but is risen!" (Luke 24:5–6).

The first to preach the Birth of Christ would be shepherds, and the first to preach His Resurrection would be the women. God speaks through the unexpected ones.

May our Lord help us to humble ourselves, that we might listen to unexpected voices. And may He grant that our voices might carry His words of encouragement and comfort to those we encounter today.

*The army of the angels appearing silenced*
*the song of shepherds' pipes.*
*And the angel uttered, Stop in the field abiding,*

*O you the governors of animals.*
*Cry out in exaltation, for Christ the*
*Lord has been born today.*
*It is His will to save the human race,*
*as God, in His good pleasure.*
—MATINS FOR DECEMBER 22

# It Was Time

ELISSA BJELETICH DAVIS

*So it was, when the angels had gone away from them into heaven, that the shepherds said to one another, "Let us now go to Bethlehem and see this thing that has come to pass, which the Lord has made known to us." And they came with haste and found Mary and Joseph, and the Babe lying in a manger. Now when they had seen Him, they made widely known the saying which was told them concerning this Child. And all those who heard it marveled at those things which were told them by the shepherds. . . . Then the shepherds returned, glorifying and praising God for all the things that they had heard and seen, as it was told them.*

—LUKE 2:15–18, 20

When the angels departed, when the great and glorious light faded, the shepherds looked at one another and dared speak.

They could not hazard disobeying the angel's directions, and surely their hearts yearned to see the Savior, Christ our Lord, wrapped in swaddling clothes.

With haste they hurried into the city, headed straight for the stables, and found, tucked away in a cave, the manger in which He so peacefully lay.

We can only imagine the scene and their reaction. Surely just this afternoon, they were ordinary shepherds, watching vigilantly over their flocks. Now, their sleep interrupted, they have received a host of angels, resplendent with God's great glory. Then back to darkness, traveling with haste through the hills—and now, once again, they are stopped in their tracks, standing before the overwhelming glory of God.

With what giddiness and joy we can only guess, they made the news widely known. They joined the angels in proclaiming that this humble newborn Child is the Christ, our salvation from above.

All those who heard it marveled at the amazing news—and perhaps also at the strangeness of the details. *Why is this great news coming to us through these lowly shepherds? And why is our Lord in a manger?*

Or perhaps God's people remembered that Moses was once a shepherd in Midian, watching over his father-in-law's flocks, when he was interrupted by an angel of the Lord. He heard God speaking from the burning bush, which—like the Theotokos—bore our fiery God but was not consumed. God heard the cries of Israel in Egypt, and *it was time:* this was the moment to send salvation, and it would begin with a humble shepherd.

In the middle of this night, again, *it was time,* and the news of it came from humble shepherds. Roused from sleep, they in turn awakened Bethlehem, proclaiming the news of our Savior's Birth.

Like Moses, these fellows are unlikely choices to communicate this most profound truth. We recall that when he was a shepherd, Moses said to the Lord, "I pray, O Lord, I am not capable," for "I am weak in speech and slow of tongue" (Ex. 4:10). He was sure that the people would not listen to him, that he was the wrong choice to lead Israel to the Promised Land. But God provided him the words. Moses didn't lead; God led through Moses. And the people followed.

When these shepherds made their proclamations in Bethlehem, perhaps God provided the words, for the people marveled at all they heard. These simple shepherds, emboldened by visions of angels and an encounter with the divine Christ Child, preached the arrival of our salvation.

*It was time* for Moses to lead Israel out of the darkness of Egypt, and *it was time* for our Lord to be proclaimed in the middle of that night. All of salvation unfolds at the right moment, in God's time. Someday the next chapter will open, when the Bridegroom arrives in the middle of the night to bring us to the banquet of the coming world.

The shepherds sleep lightly at night, alert to footfalls of predators, ready to leap into action. We too are called to vigilance, for our Lord will come for us at night, without warning (Matt. 25:13). We must be ready to rise with the shepherds at the trumpet of the angels, to greet our King.

*Shake the sleep of heedlessness from your eyes, O faithful;*
*be vigilant in prayer; shun the temptations of the evil one.*
*With the shepherds behold Christ who comes to be born:*
*Bless Him whom all creation glorifies in song.*
—VESPERS FOR DECEMBER 22

# Wonders Unfolding

ELISSA BJELETICH DAVIS

*But Mary kept all these things and pondered* them *in her heart.*

—LUKE 2:19

*And Joseph and His mother marveled at those things which were spoken of Him.*

—LUKE 2:33

How should one react when seeing the long-awaited Messiah, a tiny, vulnerable Child, asleep? Mary and Joseph are witnesses to the very Incarnation: God Himself is at rest in their arms. What a wonder, what a miracle. What words could either of them speak in that moment? Only silence—stunned, awestruck silence could follow. They must have felt as if time had frozen, as if God's plunge into our world had somehow shattered it, stilled it. Silence.

There are mornings when I wake early enough to steal some quiet time before the day unfolds. I stand in the stillness, watching my backyard awaken, and I witness miracles. Dew sparkles on blades of grass, flowers open to welcome the sunlight. My cat stalks a grasshopper. In the busy motion of my day, I don't notice wonders unfolding, but if I can be still, if I can hold my mind in silent suspension for just a few moments, I see them all around me.

Miracles are varied. Every once in a while, God sends big miracles: cancer is cured, life appears where it should not, a hopeful heart is delivered from death or pain. It's a tremendous gift to receive a miracle like that, and when we do, it's hard to be grateful *enough*, and to hold that gratitude in our minds as the moment fades and life returns to its normal rhythms.

There are smaller, but still substantial, miracles, such as when, after much prayer, a promotion is granted, or an unexpected discount comes through just in time to cover a critical expense. These gifts may not be as grand as a lifesaving intervention, but we feel the blessing deeply; we know that God is taking care of us.

And then there are those most interesting miracles that don't accomplish anything at all, practically speaking. The course of history is not changed; indeed, the course of our day might not even vary. These are the little messages of consolation, of encouragement. "I see you," He tells us with a whiff of myrrh or a bird alighting at just the right moment. "I have not forgotten you."

When God offers such a consolation, it washes over me, and for that moment at least, my heart is full. His grace fills me, and I tenderly place my hand over my heart to hold that grace inside me, if only for a moment.

We can lose that grace. We can pour it out of our hearts like milk from a cup; whether by stumbling clumsily or merely letting go our grip, we let the grace tumble out. Sometimes my cup is filled, and then I allow myself to turn my attention to some annoyance, and that little spark of anger dissipates the grace so quickly that I might not even notice its absence.

Mary must have known this. Surely she too could be still, could feel God filling her up with His grace and His love. She knew how to hold it. She could keep all these things and ponder them in her heart, turning them over to examine them gently, without crushing or relinquishing them. Both she and Joseph could pause and marvel over the things that God had done.

Can we do what they did and receive God's ineffable miracles quietly? Can we keep them a while in our hearts, rather than pouring out our cup of grace so soon? Can we learn how to ponder God's gifts not just in our minds, but in our hearts, contemplating them not just rationally, but with the eyes of the soul?

*You peoples, let us celebrate the Eve of Christ's Nativity;*
*and raising our minds on high let us*
*go up in spirit to Bethlehem;*
*and with the eyes of the soul let us look on the Virgin*
*as she hastens to give birth in a cave to*
*our God, the Lord of all things.*
*Joseph, when he looked on the greatness of His wonders,*
*thought that what he saw was a mortal,*
*wrapped in swaddling clothes as a babe;*
*but from all that came to pass he understood*
*that it was the true God,*
*who grants our souls His great mercy.*
—VESPERS FOR THE EVE OF NATIVITY, DECEMBER 24

# The Lineage of the Kingdom

ELISSA BJELETICH DAVIS

*These all died in faith, not having received the promises, but
having seen them afar off were assured of them, embraced
them and confessed that they were strangers and pilgrims on
the earth. . . . But now they desire a better, that is, a heavenly
country. Therefore God is not ashamed to be called their God,
for He has prepared a city for them.*

—HEBREWS 11:13, 16

Israel awaited its Messiah for a long, long time. The Old
Testament is full of stories of people who loved God and
packed up their belongings to follow Him to the ends of the
earth, to promised lands and safe havens. They placed themselves and their families in God's care as "strangers and pilgrims on the earth," belonging to God's Kingdom but awaiting
their King.

You and I follow God, but unlike these forebears, we have
received Christ. Our God is incarnate; He walked this earth
and suffered our sorrows and felt our joys. He gives us His Body
even now: we receive Him in Holy Communion, and He is with
us always, even until the end of the age.

We await His Return, for He shall come in glory to judge the living and the dead, and of His Kingdom there shall be no end. The waiting is hard, but perhaps not as hard as it was for those who awaited His First Coming.

God first promised to send our Savior back in the Garden, when man turned away from Paradise and death entered the world. God warned Satan that the Seed of the woman would be coming for him (Gen. 3:15). Before we were even expelled from the Garden, God was already promising that Christ would defeat death and liberate His children.

The world fell into darkness, so God baptized the earth with a Great Flood and began again. In the fullness of time, He spoke to His beloved Abraham, calling him to take up all that he loved and all that he owned and make the journey to the Promised Land. God saw that Abraham was faithful and said, "In your seed all the nations of the earth shall be blessed, because you obeyed My voice" (Gen. 22:18).

In the first chapter of his Gospel, Matthew records Christ's genealogy, which traces the fulfillment of God's promise to send the Seed. He lists the great patriarchs, whose seed God blessed, but he also lists people of more questionable character and of lower pedigree.

Tamar, who seduced her father-in-law, is there; their son Perez is part of the line of Christ. Not everyone on the list is even an Israelite, for we also see Rahab, who ran a house of ill repute in Jericho but protected and embraced the people of God.

The Church reads this genealogy on the Sunday preceding Nativity every year. After I converted to Orthodoxy, I marveled that this long list of names would be given such high priority on the calendar, as it seemed to have little to teach us.

And then one year, as I listened to Christ's genealogy, I thought about how I was born into a family line that was neither illustrious nor Christian. Around me stood Greeks and Serbs with, perhaps, a lineage like Christ's. Some can trace their ancestors back to the moment when an apostle or a great saint converted their people, and they have a thousand or more years of history as Christian families.

I don't have a Christian heritage; like Ruth, I am grafted onto this family tree. Is that why Ruth is listed? Is she there to tell us that even if we have come in from the outside, God sees us holding tight to the true Faith, and He accepts us as His children? By incorporating outsiders, the lineage demonstrates that we all have a place in the Kingdom, no matter our background or heritage.

Boaz begot Obed by Ruth, and then Obed begot Jesse, and Jesse begot David the king. Blessed David, beloved psalmist and a man after God's own heart, fathered Solomon by the wife of Uriah and cruelly sent Uriah to his death.

The lineage of Christ encompasses our humanity, the good and the bad, the familiar and the foreign. Our Lord is truly human, descended from true humans—not just the upright and virtuous, but the complicated and the hard.

God has been at work for all these thousands of years, promising and preparing and nurturing us, because He loves us. On Nativity, we celebrate the first coming of our Lord, and we continue to await the next.

*Rejoicing today, Adam is adorned with*
*the glory of divine communion,*
*as the foundation and confirmation of the wise forefathers;*
*and with him Abel leaps for joy and Enoch is glad,*
*and Seth dances together with Noah;*
*the all-praised Abraham chants with the patriarchs,*
*and from on high Melchizedek beholds a*
*birth wherein a father had no part.*
*Wherefore, celebrating the divine memory*
*of the forefathers of Christ,*
*we beseech Him that our souls may be saved.*

—VESPERS FOR THE SUNDAY BEFORE

THE NATIVITY OF CHRIST

# Sacred Places

### ELISSA BJELETICH DAVIS

*And when eight days were completed for the circumcision of the Child, His name was called JESUS, the name given by the angel before He was conceived in the womb. Now when the days of her purification according to the law of Moses were completed, they brought Him to Jerusalem to present* Him *to the Lord (as it is written in the law of the Lord, "Every male who opens the womb shall be called holy to the LORD"), and to offer a sacrifice according to what is said in the law of the Lord, "A pair of turtledoves or two young pigeons."*

—LUKE 2:21–24

The Law of Moses called for newborn sons to be circumcised on the eighth day and then presented in the temple on the fortieth. For many centuries, the people of Israel faithfully followed the Law, that their children might "be called holy to the LORD." Their physical actions manifested the spiritual reality of their desire to connect their children to God.

The temple in Jerusalem was the central locus of Jewish worship, because it was the place where God was always present and could hear the prayers and requests of His beloved people. In this physical space, the spiritual was made manifest: God sat on His throne to receive their sacrifices and hear their pleas, promising that they could always find Him there.

And so the parents brought their newborns to this point of contact, to the sacred place where the divine and the human meet, that they might be received by God.

Joseph and Mary arrived at the temple with their newborn son like so many other parents before them, but this occasion was different: these parents carried angelic proclamations quietly, pondering them in their hearts. They brought the Child who in Himself unites the divine and the human, and is therefore Himself the Temple, and they carried Him up the temple steps. Unlike the other parents, they had come to dedicate God to God, bringing not just turtledoves as a sacrifice, but truly offering the Lamb of God, who would take away the sins of the world (John 1:29).

What a profound moment, when the Temple enters the temple—when finally God enters into His own home, incarnate. He has resided, as promised, in this holy place for many centuries, and yet now here He is, present in the flesh, in a tiny human body.

Simeon and Anna, both old, both holy, awaited with Israel the coming of the Savior. Through years of prayer they had grown close to God, and they knew Him; and when He entered in the arms of His mother, they recognized this incarnate God as the selfsame God who sits on His temple throne.

At this intersection of the Old Covenant and the New, everything comes together. In this very holy place, the old ways, the Law of Moses, are fulfilled by the young mother ushering in the New Covenant by carrying in her arms the Christ Child. Old Simeon takes the young Son into his arms as a new age begins. The Sun of Righteousness dawns, and light shines into the world. Nothing is abolished; everything is fulfilled.

When we think of the Incarnation, we often think about how God took on flesh; but it is also true that our Lord entered into time and space. He entered the temple. He walked the streets of Jerusalem and Palestine; He ate and drank in people's homes and preached in synagogues. He took on *flesh*, but He also took on *place*.

We need holy places. The Israelites needed the temple. God didn't need a physical throne on the earth, but the people needed to know He was *there*—that he was *somewhere* in particular. Likewise, God did not need a body. He took on a body because we needed Him to stand with us on this actual earth, to speak with us, to enter into Hades and break open the gates of Paradise for us.

Christ is the Holy Temple. He is Himself the union of God and man, the actual place where the divine meets the human.

Even now, after our Temple has ascended to heaven and is seated in His resurrected, glorified human body at the right hand of the Father, we love our holy spaces. We travel to our churches on Sunday mornings, make pilgrimages to monasteries, and venerate myrrh-streaming icons. Like the Israelites who gravitated to the temple, we benefit from these efforts, feeling ourselves moving toward God in a tangible way.

May the Sun of Righteousness shine on our path, and may we find Him on every journey, spiritual and physical. God, be with us.

*Hail, Virgin Theotokos full of Grace,*
*for Christ our God, the Sun of Righteousness,*
*has dawned from you,*
*granting light to those in darkness.*
*And you, O Righteous Elder, rejoice,*
*taking in your arms the Deliverance of our souls,*
*who grants us resurrection.*
—APOLYTIKION OF THE PRESENTATION
OF OUR LORD, FEBRUARY 2

# A Time of Waiting

FR. MICHAEL GILLIS

*And behold, there was a man in Jerusalem whose name was Simeon, and this man was just and devout, waiting for the Consolation of Israel, and the Holy Spirit was upon him. And it had been revealed to him by the Holy Spirit that he would not see death before he had seen the Lord's Christ. So he came by the Spirit into the temple. And when the parents brought in the Child Jesus, to do for Him according to the custom of the law, he took Him up in his arms and blessed God. . . . Now there was one, Anna, a prophetess . . . of a great age . . . who did not depart from the temple, but served God with fastings and prayers night and day. And coming in that instant she gave thanks to the Lord, and spoke of Him to all those who looked for redemption in Jerusalem.*

—LUKE 2:25–28, 36–38

It's the waiting that's the worst." You often hear people say this while they are waiting for some important event. I've said it. Advent is a time of waiting.

Saint Simeon and Saint Anna the prophetess waited a lifetime. We call St. Simeon the "God-receiver" because he held in his arms Jesus as a baby, God in the flesh. The story goes that St. Simeon was one of the seventy translators of the Old

Testament into Greek, the version of the Bible we call the Septuagint. While he was translating Isaiah 7:14, he saw the words
in Hebrew, "Behold, the unmarried woman shall conceive."
Because the Hebrew word could be translated as either "virgin"
or "young woman," St. Simeon began to write "young woman,"
and suddenly an angel appeared and told him that "virgin" was
the correct translation. Further, the angel told him that he
would not die until he saw with his own eyes the Virgin and the
Messiah whom she bore.

And then St. Simeon waited. The Septuagint was translated
in the third century BC. Saint Simeon waited a long time. Some
traditions place him at 360 years old when he finally held Christ
in his arms, beholding with his own eyes the salvation of the
Lord so that he could now depart in peace.

Saint Anna the prophetess also waited. She was married as
a young woman for seven years, but after she lost her husband,
she began to live in the temple, serving God with fasting and
prayer. She was one of the women who looked after the Virgin Mary when she was brought to the temple as a young child.
Saint Anna knew Mary's life, her holiness, her virginity; so
when Mary came to the temple with Jesus in her arms to dedicate Him according to the Law on the fortieth day, Anna knew
that the little Child was none other than the Messiah, God in
the flesh, born of the Virgin, as Isaiah had prophesied and St.
Simeon had correctly translated.

Waiting is what Advent is all about. For thirty-four days now
we have been fasting, waiting for Christmas, for the Advent of
God in the flesh. And all this time the hymns we have sung in
Church have said very little about the coming Nativity. It's not

until tomorrow that we begin to sing the pre-Christmas hymns in earnest.

Thirty-four days of relative silence. Thirty-four days of waiting. Like Ss. Simeon and Anna, we do most of our waiting in silence.

When I was a child, I used to burn with anticipation for Christmas. As a child, I anticipated childish things: presents and treats and vacation from school. In fact, I don't think I have completely outgrown this childish anticipation. I hope I never do! Now, however, my anticipation is more vicarious. I share the excitement I see in the faces of the children. And as I have gotten older, I see more and more in this anticipation the longing of the whole creation for the revelation of the children of God (Rom. 8:21).

The Son of God was born of the Virgin Mary so that many children of God might be born of the virgin Church. But we are impatient. We don't want to wait; we don't want to be like Ss. Simeon and Anna. We don't want to persist in "patient continuance in doing good" (Rom. 2:7). We want the fulfillment of the promise right now.

The Son of God is born of the Virgin in secret, in a cave. God is likewise born in us as we continue in faithfulness, in virginity of heart, in secret devotion, in patient waiting. May God grant us today that we patiently continue in doing good. May God help us to wait as Ss. Simeon and Anna waited.

*See, the time of our salvation has drawn near.*
*Cave, make ready, the Virgin is drawing near to give birth.*
*Bethlehem, land of Judah, be glad and rejoice,*

*because from you our Lord has dawned.*
*Listen, mountains and hills, and lands around Judea,*
*because Christ is coming to save*
*mankind whom He fashioned,*
*for He loves mankind.*
—VESPERS FOR DECEMBER 19

# Becoming a True Human Being

FR. MICHAEL GILLIS

*Now the virginity of Mary was hidden from the prince of this world, as was also her offspring, and the death of the Lord; three mysteries of renown, which were wrought in silence by God. How, then, was He manifested to the world? A star shone forth in heaven above all the other stars, the light of which was inexpressible, while its novelty struck men with astonishment. And all the rest of the stars, with the sun and moon, formed a chorus to this star, and its light was exceedingly great above them all. And there was agitation felt as to whence this new spectacle came, so unlike to everything else [in the heavens]. Hence every kind of magic was destroyed, and every bond of wickedness disappeared; ignorance was removed, and the old kingdom abolished, God Himself being manifested in human form for the renewal of eternal life. And now that took a beginning which had been prepared by God. Henceforth all things were in a state of tumult, because He meditated the abolition of death.*

—ST. IGNATIUS OF ANTIOCH, LETTER

TO THE EPHESIANS, 19:1–3[15]

Today, on the feast day of St. Ignatius of Antioch, the Church begins chanting the pre-festal hymns of Christ's

Nativity. Saint Ignatius was the bishop of Antioch at the end of the first and the beginning of the second centuries AD, famously martyred in the arena by being devoured by wild animals. On the way to his death in Rome, he wrote letters to the churches in the cities along his route. The letters stressed the importance of obedience and gentleness as well as the concrete reality of all the events in the life of Jesus Christ. A real star shone in the sky to announce the real Birth of the God-man to the Virgin. He really lived and really died and really rose again. Jesus Christ was a true human being.

In his letters, St. Ignatius also stressed one more point that might seem strange to us today: he asked the Christians along the way, especially those living in Rome, not to hinder his martyrdom. Saint Ignatius told them he had not yet become a true disciple of Christ; he was not yet a true human being. He would not become a true disciple of Christ, and thus a true human being, until he followed Christ all the way to his death.

Saint Paul tells us that we must put on the new man, birthed in us at baptism. This new human being is none other than our Lord Jesus Christ (Eph. 4:20–24). The Logos of God clothed Himself in humanity at the Incarnation, thus forming the new man, or the true human being, whom we put on. As we take off the vices, as if they were clothing, and put on the virtues, we are clothed in Christ—we are becoming true human beings.

This is a daily, even hourly, spiritual exercise of taking off the old person and putting on the new. It is a process of transformation that takes a lifetime and is only completed in our death. This is why Orthodox Christians seldom confidently declare that they are saved. Jesus said, "He who endures to the end will be saved" (Matt. 10:22). Saint Ignatius knew this and would not rest on his past record as a holy bishop and a prisoner for Christ. He knew that to be saved he must be faithful to Christ even to the end. Only then would he fully put on Christ, the true Human Being; and only in being faithful to our last breath do we become true human beings.

But how do we do it? How do we take off the old and put on the new? We take off the old man as we resist temptation, as we say "no" to our impulses, fleshly desires, and fears. We take off the old when we fast, when we control ourselves, and when we ourselves suffer so that others may not suffer.

Putting on the new man means acquiring virtues, allowing our minds to be renewed, and forgiving those who have offended us. Another name for virtue is the fruit of the Spirit. These fruits include—but are not limited to—love, joy, peace, patience, kindness, gentleness, faith, goodness, and self-control. When we acquire these virtues, we become more like Christ and thus become more ourselves and truer human beings.

Saint Ignatius did not suddenly become a saint at his martyrdom. Rather, his martyrdom revealed him as a saint. Similarly, the big events of our life do not make us who we are as much as they *reveal* who we are. It's really the little things that change us. It's the faithfulness in the daily disciplines that changes us. It's loving the people who are in our lives every day that makes us holy. And as we continue faithfully to the end, then we too will be martyrs for Christ. Like St. Ignatius, we will be true human beings.

*Shining forth like a star from the East,*
*you illumined the world.*
*Resplendent in the rays of your discourses,*
*you drove away the darkness,*
*and like Paul valiantly finished the race,*
*enduring tribulations among the nations and in the cities.*
*Wherefore, like wheat you were ground*
*by the teeth of wild beasts*
*as an offering for your Lord. O blessed God-bearer Ignatius,*
*entreat Christ God that He may grant*
*remission of transgressions*
*unto those who honor your holy memory with love.*

—MATINS FOR DECEMBER 20

# Acquiring Humility

FR. MICHAEL GILLIS

*Let this mind be in you which was also in Christ Jesus, who, being in the form of God, did not consider it robbery to be equal with God, but made Himself of no reputation, taking the form of a bondservant, and coming in the likeness of men.*

—PHILIPPIANS 2:5–7

When God became human for our sakes, He revealed one of His most essential qualities: humility. Consequently, as we acquire virtues through repentance and the transformation of our minds, one of the central virtues we must acquire is humility. It is the fruit of theosis and reveals nothing less than the character of Jesus Christ in us.

There is an interesting irony in the spiritual life: the greatest saints see themselves as the worst of sinners. How can this be? This happens because as we are transformed into the image of Christ by the grace of God and through ascetic practice, we acquire humility. The humble person does not compare himself with others, for the humble person assumes everyone else is better (Phil. 2:3). Therefore, the humble person sees only his or her own sin. As we draw nearer to God, we become much more aware of the magnitude of His love and mercy. And in the face of God's great love and mercy, even very small sins seem too big.

But where do we begin? How do we begin to acquire humility, and how do we know if we are acquiring it? Someone once said that humility is not thinking less of yourself; it's thinking of yourself less. Probably one of the clearest signs that we are acquiring true humility is that we spend much less time thinking about ourselves and much more time and energy thinking and caring about God and other people. Another sign of humility is that we are not comparing ourselves with anyone except Jesus. And finally, true humility judges and condemns no one.

It is said of St. Moses the Ethiopian that he was a man of tall body and lowly soul. Once St. Moses was very distressed because he was called to a meeting with the brother monks to judge one who had gravely sinned. When he came to the meeting place, he entered the room saying nothing but carrying a bag of sand with a hole in it, leaving a trail of sand behind him. Saint Moses was a very famous monk, so the brother monks wanted to know what he meant by this. Finally he said, "You called me here to judge my brother whom I can see, but my own sins leave a trail behind me that I cannot see." Then the brothers said nothing more against the brother who had sinned, but rather, forgave him.

When we look at the saints, we see many excellent examples of humility; but when I look at my own life, I see that I am very far from acquiring it. Where does someone like me begin? Thankfully, the Holy Fathers of the Church have left us instructions on the matter. Although there are many paths, the Fathers mention the ascetical practice of obedience—or not doing our own will—as a means to acquire humility.

However, obedience can be a tricky asceticism to practice for those who do not live in monasteries. In a monastery, a monk obeys only one authority: the abbot. However, those of us in the world have many authorities in our lives: government, church, and work authorities, as well as many family obligations. These authorities often can be contradictory and even abusive, so how can we know which to obey? I think the key lies in not doing our own will and in following the advice of trusted sources when we are not sure.

Saint Isaac the Syrian said that no one can acquire humility except by humility's own means. Not doing our own will is an ascetic practice we can enter into—a practice that the Fathers of the Church tell us will help. But at the end of the day, only God can transform us. Only God knows what we need to be saved.

*Looking to Christ, who humbles Himself,*
*let us be lifted up from the passions that seek the ground;*
*with good zeal trained by faith not to think lofty things,*
*let us be humbled in spirit;*
*that by works which exalt we may exalt*
*the One who is being brought forth.*
—VESPERS FOR DECEMBER 19

# Miracles as Signs

### FR. MICHAEL GILLIS

*And when John had heard in prison about the works of Christ, he sent two of his disciples and said to Him, "Are You the Coming One, or do we look for another?" Jesus answered and said to them, "Go and tell John the things which you hear and see: The blind see and the lame walk; the lepers are cleansed and the deaf hear; the dead are raised up and the poor have the gospel preached to them. And blessed is he who is not offended because of Me."*

—MATTHEW 11:2–6

Saint John Chrysostom points out that every person whom Jesus healed later got sick again and died. Throughout His ministry, Jesus healed thousands of people, but none of them stayed healthy very long. That's because the real human problem is not sickness, but death; and death can only be healed through death. So we might ask the question, "Why did Jesus heal all those people if they were only going to get sick again and die anyway?"

Nowadays, when we look at the healings Jesus performed, we call them miracles. This is completely misleading. The word *miracle* refers to something unexplainable, out of the ordinary. But Jesus' healings are not called miracles in the Bible; the Gospel writers call them *signs*. A sign points to something. John the Baptist heard of the works Jesus was doing but did not see signs. Perhaps John was only looking at the miracles as amazing feats and did not see that they pointed to Jesus as the Messiah. So he sent two of his disciples to ask Jesus plainly, "Are you the Coming One, or do we look for another?"

Jesus answered by paraphrasing the words of the prophet Isaiah: "*The* blind see and *the* lame walk; *the* lepers are cleansed and *the* deaf hear; *the* dead are raised up and *the* poor have the gospel preached to them." Everything that Jesus is doing points to something. Every amazing miracle has a meaning. And it's this meaning that John is missing—that we all tend to miss. The miracles themselves are shouting, "Here is the Messiah! Here is the Son of God! Pay attention to My words, to My life, to My death; for they are the words, life, and even death of God."

Maybe that's why Jesus had to add the final phrase, "And blessed is he who is not offended because of Me." That Jesus is a prophet is not hard to believe. But that Jesus is God? That God Himself has come as a Man? Well, that's just offensive. It's offensive because we think we already know what the coming of God would be like, and it certainly is not in the form of a human being who sweats and sleeps and weeps and bleeds. And yet, here is a Man doing what only God can do.

It would be a silly thing if I drove past a stop sign admiring how well it was designed and placed, yet not actually stopping. But this is what we tend to do when it comes to miracles, to the signs that God gives us throughout our lives. Most of us never experience something as dramatic as an irrefutable miracle. No, for most of us God mercifully grants us small wonders, amazing coincidences, and mysterious indicators that point beyond themselves to the One we need to pay attention to.

Saint Anthony the Great said that the whole universe is the Word of God written in very large letters. The signs are everywhere, pointing to the One we are looking for—if indeed we are looking for Him. Maybe we are just looking for the next amazing thing, the next beautiful or wonderful thing, instead of looking for the amazing, beautiful, and wonderful One. Perhaps that's our problem. It's not that we see no signs, or that the signs are not wonderful or amazing enough. No, our problem is that we are admiring the signs, but not looking to and admiring Him to whom they point.

*Fulfilling the oracles and visions of the prophets,*
*the Word is brought to birth in flesh and becomes corporeal,*
*and after birth he is laid in a manger of irrational beasts.*
*This is the supreme condescension! This*
*the awesome dispensation!*
*For this we sing: The King of Israel, Christ, draws near.*
—MATINS FOR DECEMBER 21

# Mercy & Truth Together

FR. MICHAEL GILLIS

*Show us Your mercy, O Lord,*
*And grant us Your salvation.*
*I will hear what the Lord God will speak in me,*
*For He will speak peace*
*To His people and to His Holy ones,*
*And to those who turn their heart to Him.*
*His salvation is very close at hand to those who fear Him,*
*That glory may dwell in our land.*
*Mercy and truth met together;*
*Righteousness and peace kissed each other;*
*Truth arose from the earth,*
*And righteousness looked down from heaven.*
*For the Lord will give goodness,*
*And our land shall yield its fruit.*
*Righteousness shall go before Him*
*And establish His footsteps as our pathway.*

—PSALM 84/85:8–14

The world has always been much more interested in truth than in mercy, more interested in righteousness/justice than in peace. (The biblical word translated "righteousness" can also be translated as "justice.") But the psalmist tells us that in the coming Kingdom of the Messiah, mercy and truth will meet, and righteousness/justice and peace will kiss each other.

I think one of the reasons I tend to emphasize truth and righteousness over mercy and peace is that I tend to think I am usually right—that my perspective is the true one. But many of the Church Fathers have noted that heresy is often the overemphasis of one truth against other truths. Similarly, we err when we emphasize truth itself over mercy or justice over peace. Jesus is Truth (John 14:6), and He is very compassionate and merciful (James 5:11). Jesus is the Sun of Righteousness (Mal. 3:20/4:2), and He gives us His peace (John 14:27).

The Baby in the manger teaches us that only humility can bring truth and mercy, justice and peace together. Only when we humble ourselves, knowing that God is at work in the world in many more ways than are evident to us, can we begin to bring truth and mercy together. When we demand the truth without showing mercy, we pervert the truth; when we seek justice but there is no peace, we are only making a mockery of the very righteousness we are seeking.

When I began my ordained ministry as a deacon doing youth work, I did not know my measure. I used to think I knew how to help people repent and find Christ. I would look at people, their lives and their situations, and it would seem obvious to me what they needed to do to turn things around. I could quote chapter and verse from the Bible and from the holy canons and from the Fathers. I knew the truth; I knew what was right and just—or so I thought.

I became a generator of "shoulds" in people's lives: "You should pray more; you should fast this way; you should discipline your children this way; you should come to church earlier and more often." I had all the arguments, the quotations, the reasons my "shoulds" were true, my "shoulds" were right. It would be years later that I discovered how unhelpful and potentially harmful "shoulds" are.

The turning point for me came when I wrestled with my own prayer rule. I had been struggling for years to pray as I "should." I had adopted various rules that would never last very long. Finally, I asked my spiritual father. I was afraid to do this; it took a few years' worth of visits to get up the courage to ask. I was sure that he would assign me an hour-long rule that I could never complete. However, I was desperate.

And so I asked. Immediately he responded with a rule that takes only ten minutes to complete—if I say it slowly and meditatively, as he asked me to say it. But I could crank it out in five minutes or less in a pinch.

I protested a little that the rule was too short. He told me it was a mercy, but if I just did it, I would find peace. And so I just did it. The results surprised me. Instead of my prayer times being a guilt-filled slog, I could easily complete my rule and very often added more, just because I wanted to stay in that peaceful place. When I was in a hurry, I could rush through and spend the day without guilt.

This experience began to change the way I spoke to others about truth and justice. Instead of thinking only about what is true, I also thought about what is merciful. Instead of thinking only about encouraging righteousness in my spiritual children, I looked for what resulted in peace (Rom. 14:19). And I began to discover that when truth is mixed with mercy, indeed "the souls of the righteous are adorned" with peace.

*Adorn yourself well, O Bethlehem, for Eden has been opened!*
*Prepare yourself, O Ephratha, for Adam*
*has been restored, and Eve with him:*
*for the curse has been annulled, salvation has blossomed forth,*
*and the souls of the righteous are adorned,*
*offering hymnody instead of myrrh as their gift,*
*and receiving salvation of soul and incorruption.*
*For, lo! He who lies in the manger orders those who cry out*
*to chant unceasingly in spirit: Glory be to You, O Lord!*
—VESPERS FOR DECEMBER 23

# Awe & Wonder

### FR. MICHAEL GILLIS

*O Lord, our Lord, how wondrous is Your name*
*    in all the earth,*
*For Your splendor is exalted far beyond the heavens.*
*From the mouths of babies and nursing infants*
*You prepared praise because of Your enemies,*
*That You may destroy the enemy and avenger.*
*For I shall look at the heavens, the works of Your fingers,*
*The moon and stars You established.*
*What is man that You remember him,*
*Or the son of man that You visit him?*

—PSALM 8:1–4

Saint Isaac the Syrian notes that the experience of awe and wonder can be the same thing as prayer. When we are filled with awe and wonder, our hearts are opened and our awareness of the ever-present God is heightened. To be filled with awe and wonder is the closest thing to heaven that we can experience on earth.

Even our secular culture remembers awe and wonder at Christmastime—or they try to revive the memory of it in order to sell a few more widgets and toys and sweaters. It seems that children are the only ones who still experience awe and wonder—at least, children are the only ones who are expected to experience it until it is educated out of them.

In my first year of college, I took an astronomy course because it seemed the easiest lab science I could get away with. While studying the stars and planets, I was amazed again and again, despite my professor's best efforts to educate amazement out of me. I was awed by the size, the clockwork movement, and the sheer impossibility of biological life in our universe. At that time, I was a devout Christian of the Jesus Movement type, and to me going to astronomy class was like going to church. I walked away from every lecture amazed at the miracle of it all, at the greatness of God.

And it is tonight, on Christmas Eve, that the whole world was amazed at a star. Historians tell us the star shone for quite a long time—long enough for wise men, astrologers from the East, to follow it and visit the Baby King whom the star portended. But this night, it was particularly the shepherds keeping watch over their flocks whose turn it was to be amazed. Suddenly, the sky was filled with angels singing, "Glory to God in the highest, and on earth peace, goodwill toward men!" (Luke 2:14). The shepherds, full of awe and wonder, went to Bethlehem to find a Baby and to wonder still more at the sight: a King born in a cave.

And we still wonder today. God on high humbled Himself and became man, but without change. God became man without ceasing to be God, yet assuming everything that is human except sin. Out of love for His fallen creatures, the Creator of the universe limits Himself to the bubble of creation that can sustain biological life. He limits Himself to human form, limits Himself to become a first-century Jew in Palestine under

Roman occupation, limits Himself to be a Baby nursing at His mother's breast, all without ceasing to be the Creator and Sustainer of all: awe and wonder.

To tell the truth, I love all the trappings of secular Christmas. I love the decorations and the trees and the carols and the presents. I love the look in the eyes of children—the wonder, the awe. And even though I know it is mostly just a base commercialization of an idealized and secularized tradition that never actually existed except in novels and TV specials, still I love it. I love it because Christmas season encourages us all to wonder. It's a time when it's okay to dial down the rational part of our minds a bit and just be in awe, just wonder at it all.

And secretly, in my heart, I see all the outward show as just an excuse, an opportunity to express my inner wonder and awe at the love of God. The lights on the tree are for the Light of the world. The carols I hum are for the song in my heart. The gifts for my family and friends are just tokens of my love—and more so, of God's love for us all.

Merry Christmas!

*Behold, the time of our salvation has drawn near!*
*Prepare yourself, O cave: the Virgin approaches to give birth!*
*O Bethlehem, you land of Judah, adorn yourself and be glad,*
*for our Lord has shone forth from you!*
*Hearken, you mountains and hills, and*
*you, lands of Judea round about:*
*for Christ comes, that He might save*
*man whom He had created,*
*in that He loves mankind!*
—VESPERS FOR DECEMBER 24

# From Self-Will to Resurrection Life

### FR. MICHAEL GILLIS

*For unto us a Child is born, unto us a Son is given; and the government will be upon His shoulder. His name will be called the Angel of Great Counsel, for I shall bring peace upon the rulers, peace and health by Him. Great shall be His government, and of His peace there is no end. His peace shall be upon the throne of David and over His kingdom, to order and establish it with righteousness and judgment, from that time forward and unto ages of ages. The zeal of the Lord of hosts shall perform this.*

—ISAIAH 9:5–6

Christ is born! Glorify Him! Christ is come from heaven! Receive Him! Christ is on earth! Be lifted up!

When God dwells with human beings, all of humanity is lifted to a higher place, a new place. Death, which had been our overlord, trembles. Life has joined Himself to humanity. The New Eve has given birth to the New Adam.

The Birth of Jesus manifests the beginning of our transformation. Before God became man, humanity was bound by death. But God begins to destroy its power by joining Life to the human race, which had become corrupted by death. Now human beings have a choice. Now human beings can choose Life.

However, to choose Life is to choose the way of the Life-giver. The way of the Life-giver is the way of voluntary death out of love: the mystery of the Cross. In the icon of the Nativity of our Lord, we see the Baby Jesus lying in a manger in a cave. If you look closely at the manger in traditional Orthodox icons, it is a small sarcophagus or stone coffin. And the swaddling clothes are strips of cloth like those used to preserve a dead body, as in the icon of the raising of Lazarus. Jesus is God become Man, born to die out of love for humankind.

For most of us, the struggle against death takes place in our struggle to submit our will to God. Like Eve in the Garden, we want our own will; we want what seems best to us. And consequently, we choose death—ignorantly, perhaps. Not realizing what we are doing, we seek to promote our self-will and thus choose death. The habits of our ancestors are hard to break.

But Jesus as the New Adam has made a way for us, a way to return from death to Life. It is a way that requires us to crucify our self-will out of love for others. It is a way that calls us to love our neighbor as ourselves, even to love our enemy. This narrow way that Jesus has called us to is the way of Life because it is the way of Jesus; it is the way by which we lose our life to find it. And in finding our life in Christ, we are transfigured day by day into His likeness.

Like every other Christian, I too struggle to follow Christ by laying down my self-will out of love for others. As I have reflected over the years on my many failures, I have come to the conclusion that I often do not believe that God is really God.

That is, I don't really believe that He is the God of my circumstances, that the trials and tribulations that come my way are
from His hand.

Now certainly, troubles come my way because of my sinful
choices, by the sinful choices of the people around me, and the
choices all human beings have made since our ancestors' expul-
sion from Paradise. Death and suffering, trials and tribulations
are the result of human sin. However—and this is the deep
mystery of God being God—no trial or tribulation, nor even
death or suffering, can come to me from human sin if it is not
also from the hand of God. As Jesus said to Pontius Pilate, "You
could have no power at all against Me unless it had been given
you from above" (John 19:11). That's why Jesus could say in
the Garden of Gethsemane, "Not My will, but Yours, be done"
(Luke 22:42).

Out of love for humanity, Jesus became human that He might
fully follow the will of His Father, even to the point of being
executed by sinful men. However, because God is God, death
offered out of love becomes Resurrection. We too, following
Jesus' example, die daily, laying down our self-will out of love for
others. And miracle of miracles, we too experience resurrection
life, even while still living in this body of death.

*For a child was born,*
*a Son, from Adam's nature, and given*
*unto those who believe in Him.*
*Of the age to come He is Father and Prince,*
*and His name has been called the Angel of Great Counsel.*
*Mighty God is He; wonderful Counselor, Prince of peace,*

*and He governs creation with authority.*
—MATINS FOR THE NATIVITY OF OUR
LORD JESUS CHRIST, DECEMBER 25

# God Is in the Mess

### NICOLE M. ROCCAS

*But I make known to you, brethren, that the gospel which was preached by me is not according to man. For I neither received it from man, nor was I taught it, but it came through the revelation of Jesus Christ.*

—GALATIANS 1:11–12

He knew this virgin would be trouble. Hadn't he said as much at the temple when the lot had fallen on him to take her in?

"I am an old man, and she is a young girl!" Joseph had protested (Prot. Jas. 9).[16] What did it matter if this virgin needed protection? Taking her in would make him the local laughingstock.

Still, the priest had been adamant. "Fear the Lord, O Joseph," he'd scolded the old man.

And so, anxious to avoid the wrath of God, Joseph took Mary in. To help guard against scandal, he gave her a home in one of his buildings, where she worked and spun fine silk to be used in the temple (see Prot. Jas. 11–12).

But all that had been wishful thinking, he realized. Now the woman was, unthinkably, pregnant. To make matters worse, instead of admitting her transgression, she kept blaspheming the Lord by claiming it was *His* son.

Joseph had always tried to be a decent and faithful man— toward God, toward kin, toward fellow man—only to see this disgrace soil what were supposed to be the golden years of his life. The anguish and shame were enough to swallow him whole.

These emotions are captured in the Nativity icon. We find Joseph brooding in the bottom corner, forming a tableau that clashes with the exaltation permeating the rest of the scene.

Huddled alone on a rock, his chin a burden in his hands, a haggard Joseph ruminates over the scandal. But even though Joseph was unable to wrap his mind around the mystery of the Incarnation, he was equally unwilling to draw further attention to Mary or himself by publicizing her disgrace. Caught in an impossible situation, Joseph is overtaken by a dark despair that is sometimes personified in icons as a shadowy interlocutor meant to represent Satan.

Joseph's despondency is a microcosm of our own human inability to grasp how the love of God could possibly manifest itself within the messy, flesh-and-bone fabric of earthly existence. And, like Joseph, for many of us fewer areas of life seem more incompatible with the Incarnation than our families, our marriages.

Today, the Sunday after Christmas, is devoted to some of the members of Christ's earthly family. Along with Joseph the Betrothed, we remember David the Prophet and James, the Brother of our Lord. In grouping these holy men together like this, it's easy to paint a one-sided, triumphal picture of Christ's family. Yet reading against the grain of their lives recalls another story.

In a season that, more than any other, tempts us to project false, idyllic versions of family life onto those around us, it's almost as though the Church is reminding us that no family is perfect, not even that of Jesus. His ancestor David was a murderer and adulterer before his repentance. His own mother's betrothed considered abandoning them both before he overcame doubt and honored the Christ Child. While we revere Joseph as a faithful adoptive father to Christ, whispers of his and Mary's old shame never disappeared. Even decades later, after Jesus had performed miracle upon miracle, those familiar with His family could only sneer. "Is this not the carpenter's son?" they scoffed. "Is not His mother called Mary?" (Matt. 13:55).

And yet, just as this Sunday reminds us that no family is perfect, it also bears witness to the reality that no family is fully outside the bounds of God's grace and mercy. God brought salvation into the world through a family in Nazareth whose righteousness was hidden from the sight of others, and He is alive and at work in our own families, as well as in the painful memories we may still carry *from* those families. As today's verses remind us, the Good News Christ embodied on entering this world is not the gospel of man—that is, it doesn't behave according to what we expect in the earthly frame. It is bigger and more mysterious than that.

May we cling to Christ in the midst of our own despair and darkness, and may He never cease to reveal His love in the woundedness that encompasses us.

*O Joseph, proclaim the glad tidings to*
*David, the ancestor of God,*
*For you have seen a Virgin give birth;*
*with the shepherds you gave glory;*

*with the Magi you worshipped;*
*by an angel were you instructed.*
*Entreat Christ God that He may save our souls!*
—VESPERS FOR THE SUNDAY AFTER NATIVITY

# The Example of the Theotokos

NICOLE M. ROCCAS

*Now Moses was tending the sheep of Jethro his father-in-law, the priest of Midian. Then he led them to the back of the desert and came to Horeb, the mountain of God. Then the Angel of the Lord appeared to him in a flame of fire from the midst of a bush.*

—EXODUS 3:1–2

When I was growing up, a small pink plaque hung on the wall outside my bedroom, printed with a nineteenth-century nursery rhyme:

What are little girls made of?
Sugar and spice and everything nice.
That's what little girls are made of.

The saccharine lines were emblematic of what it meant to be a "good girl" (and, later, woman) in the various spheres of my life back then. Whether in church, at school, or with my family, I was expected to be nice, docile, and above all, submissive. Even in the face of evil. Even when it might mean losing myself, or rather, never fully developing a distinct sense of self to lose in the first place.

That plaque always bothered me. Why didn't my brothers have to shrink and silence and sweeten themselves the way I was expected to? Its words burrowed inside me in ways that are hard to shake. To this day, when I stand up for myself, or use too firm a voice or too many big words in a sentence, the pink plaque often flashes before my eyes, filling me with the shame of not measuring up, of straying outside the lines, of failing to embody the *sugar-and-spice-and-everything-nice* standard.

I wonder how different my formative concepts of womanhood would have been if, instead of that plaque, we'd had an icon of the Theotokos hanging in the hallway. While Mary modeled the qualities of holy womanhood—purity, faithfulness, attentiveness to the voice of God—she was *not* made of sugar and spice and everything nice. Thank God.

When the angel entreats her to bear the Son of God in her womb, Mary does not simply smile and comply. Instead, she asks a question: "How can this be, since I do not know a man?" (Luke 1:34). In other words: How can God make this request of me, given who I am? In being an active, even insistent, actor in the conversation and the Annunciation, Mary not only proclaims the Virgin Birth for the first time, but also embodies a holiness that is participatory, inquisitive—even bold. In the end, she steps into her role as the birthgiver of God not out of coercion, but out of volition: "Let it be to me according to your word" (Luke 1:38).

Now, nine months later as we behold the Birth of Christ, we find that the will of God has preserved the qualities that make her unique, exceptional. The very aspect of her selfhood that Mary asserted at the Annunciation—her virginity—has been retained.

The hymn for today likens Mary's womb to the bush that burned without being consumed. Even while welcoming the Son of the eternal God into her womb, Mary still remained Mary—a virgin, yes, but more than that, the person she was, and remains.

As the Mother of God, Mary is—as all of us are called to be— also her own person who, in exercising her God-given free will for His glory, challenges our concepts of what it means to be "good." Years later she will prod her Son to see that more wine is served to guests at the wedding of Cana (John 2:1–11), ushering in the start of Jesus' public ministry. The vignette is another reminder that holiness is not synonymous with niceness or passivity.

Today is the Synaxis, or meeting, of the Theotokos. Although I was not guided by her icon and example as a young girl, I can still "meet" her today. In drawing near to her, I can remember that cooperating with the will of God is not about losing myself but rather about allowing my truest self to be transformed and actualized in the light of God's glory.

For someone who learned early that being a "good girl" (and by extension woman) meant silencing the capacity to act boldly and freely, the icon of womanhood—really, of humanity—we find in the Theotokos is good news indeed.

*Your sacred womb, which was depicted by the bush*
*which burned without being consumed,*
*manifestly bore the Word and mingled*
*God with a human image,*
*loosing the wretched womb of Eve from the bitter curse of old.*
*Let us glorify Him, O you mortals!*
—MATINS FOR DECEMBER 25

# The Joy of Christmas & the Pain of the Cross

NICOLE M. ROCCAS

*When they heard these things they were cut to the heart, and they gnashed at [Stephen] with their teeth. But he, being full of the Holy Spirit, gazed into heaven and saw the glory of God, and Jesus standing at the right hand of God, and said, "Look! I see the heavens opened and the Son of Man standing at the right hand of God!" Then they cried out with a loud voice, stopped their ears, and ran at him with one accord; and they cast him out of the city and stoned him.*

—ACTS 7:54–58

I never know what to make of yard signs or social media rants that insist we "Keep Christ in Christmas!" Not that I'd prefer to keep Christ out of it; I'm just not sure whether most of us—myself included—are prepared to live up to such an injunction. Is it truly Christ we want, or just a nostalgic manger scene to conjure up rose-colored memories of the supposed good old days?

Today, the commemoration of St. Stephen, the first martyr of the New Testament Church, is a good day to sit with this question. It is the first of a three-day series that recalls some of the bloodiest events in Christian history. Tomorrow, December 28, we remember the twenty thousand martyrs of Nicomedia in the fourth century, and the next day, the slaughter of the Holy Innocents during the reign of King Herod. All three are immoveable commemorations—they are always observed right after Christmas.

This connection between Christmas and martyric holy days is a whisper of wisdom from historical Christianity, reminding us we ought never to separate the joy of Christmas from the pain of the Cross, the death toward which all our lives are oriented as we seek to follow Christ.

In the early centuries of the Church, the Incarnation was closely associated not with Christ's Birth—His entrance into the world of flesh—but instead with His death on the Cross. Indeed, very little concerning the Christmas narrative is found in St. Athanasius's *On the Incarnation*, one of the most vital early Church texts to expound on Christ's human nature.

For Athanasius, as miraculous as Jesus' incarnational Birth was, taking on flesh wasn't the ultimate point. Christ, he wrote, "did not simply will to become embodied." He came into the world to save sinners through a sacrificial death. But for Christ—the immortal Son of God—to accomplish that, He had to have a body that was able to die.

And so, continues Athanasius:

He takes to Himself a body capable of death, that it, by partaking of the Word who is above all, might be worthy to die in the stead of all, and might, because of the Word which had come to dwell in it, remain incorruptible, and that thenceforth corruption might be stayed from all by the grace of the Resurrection.[17]

When we remember St. Stephen the Protomartyr, we also remember that Christmas is more than an occasion for joy, childlikeness, and festivity. It is the cause of sacred sorrow, resistance, and bloodshed. It is the guttural ache of a creation toward its Savior. It is the first, tremulous foreshock of the earthquake that will culminate on Holy Friday, when the temple curtain is torn in two. It is the beginning of the road to the Cross.

But it is also the beginning of the Resurrection. If the Cross is the reason for Christ's Birth, then the Resurrection is the reason for the Cross:

> For now that He has come to our realm, and taken up His abode in one body among His peers, henceforth the whole conspiracy of the enemy against mankind is checked, and the corruption of death which before was prevailing against them is done away. For the race of men had gone to ruin, had not the Lord and Saviour of all, the Son of God, come among us to meet the end of death.[18]

Perhaps this Nativity season, instead of calling on others to keep Christ in Christmas, we might endeavor within ourselves, in the peace and hope of the Resurrection, to keep the Cross in Christmas.

*Having enlightened your thought with the grace of the Spirit,*
*You did appear like an angel in countenance, O Stephen,*

*your body, luminous with inner splendor,*
*emitting spiritual radiance upon those who beheld you,*
*for which cause you received a vision of light,*
*for the heavens were most gloriously opened to you,*
*you first among martyrs and their boast.*
—VESPERS FOR DECEMBER 27

# "A Map We Carry in Our Hearts"

NICOLE M. ROCCAS

*Then Herod, when he had secretly called the wise men, determined from them what time the star appeared. And he sent them to Bethlehem and said, "Go and search carefully for the young Child, and when you have found Him, bring back word to me, that I may come and worship Him also."*

—MATTHEW 2:7–8

Some days and commemorations on the Christian calendar feel well-worn and well-trodden, like footpaths that tame the anarchic wilderness of time—the twelve great feasts of the year, for example, or the feasts of familiar saints and holy days. Other days seem almost foreign, taking us off the beaten paths of sacred time toward something . . . deeper? More obscure? Mysterious?

If you're like me, today is one of those days. Falling between the cracks of the more familiar martyric holy days of St. Stephen (December 27) and the Holy Innocents (December 29), December 28 recalls the twenty thousand martyrs who, in the early fourth century, were executed inside their church in Nicomedia after refusing to renounce Christ. The icon for this event depicts a small, enclosed church reminiscent of the ark of Noah. Instead of floating in the waters of the great Flood, however, the church hovers above a bed of burning logs; its inhabitants were burned alive at Emperor Maximian's command.

It's a lot to take in, especially in a week that is already laden with some of the most heartbreaking accounts of bloodshed in Christian history—and all of this, somewhat confusingly, in the midst of the post-Nativity festal period, the longest fast-free period of the Orthodox year. It's difficult to keep it all straight. Perhaps this is why the twenty thousand martyrs tend to fall off the radar of our temporal awareness. Few churches hold liturgies to commemorate this event, and likely even fewer of us do so in our homes.

But I think this omission goes deeper than simple busyness or the difficulty of juggling all the competing liturgical themes in the wake of Christ's Nativity. Personally, during the days after Christmas I frequently struggle with a kind of spiritual "compassion fatigue." Not only am I exhausted by days or even weeks of tending to family, loved ones, fasting, feasting, gifts, and church services. I also—on some level, at least—am weary from trying to care about *all* the post-Nativity martyrs and tragedies. Is a break too much to ask for? A day where we just take a quick breather from all the saints and commemorations?

This is the part where I should offer some practical application or "hack" to help us all tend to the Orthodox calendar in a deeper way. But such an ambitious goal strikes me as impossible for most of us, and maybe that's the takeaway.

Maybe when we find ourselves unable to fully take in all the death and suffering recalled throughout the Orthodox year, it's enough, for now, to recognize our fatigue, our finite attention, our feeble efforts.

Maybe the Orthodox calendar—its breadth, its multivalence, its inability to be fully tamed or accomplished—is not a to-do list we finally get through, but a banquet whose endless sumptuous dishes we can never finish tasting.

Maybe our journey is less about grasping the *content* of what we commemorate every day of the sacred year and more about progressively tuning and re-tuning our hearts to its *form*, learning to pattern our lives according to a salvific story that extends beyond ourselves, even when certain scenes in that story feel strange or unfamiliar.

The calendar is not a textbook we memorize for a test, but—as theologian James K. A. Smith describes it—it is "a map we carry in our hearts." Its practices are "disciplines of attunement that calibrate the spiritual timekeeping we carry in our bones, ... [enabling] us to live as a futural people animated by hope."[19]

Approaching today through this lens relieves the pressure and replaces it with a kind of spaciousness—curiosity, even. Compassion-fatigued or not, I can sample this new dish I've encountered in the vast potluck of sacred time—remembering the twenty thousand martyrs of Nicomedia. I can give thanks to God, ask for the holy prayers of these unfamiliar saints, and at least for a few moments revere the time I so often overlook or fail to notice, whether out of limitation or out of my preference for familiarity.

Glory to God for all things, and all times.

*A twenty-thousand numbered battalion of martyrs*
*arises like an unwaning star great with brightness,*
*enlightening by faith the hearts and*
*the minds of all godly folk.*
*For, enkindled with divine love unto the Master,*
*this courageous host received a sanctified ending*
*when eagerly burned with fire.*
—KONTAKION FOR DECEMBER 28

# Container of the Uncontainable

### NICOLE M. ROCCAS

*Then Herod, when he saw that he was deceived by the wise men, was exceedingly angry; and he sent forth and put to death all the male children who were in Bethlehem and in all its districts, from two years old and under, according to the time which he had determined from the wise men. Then was fulfilled what was spoken by Jeremiah the prophet, saying:*

*"A voice was heard in Ramah,*
*Lamentation, weeping, and great mourning,*
*Rachel weeping for her children,*
*Refusing to be comforted,*
*Because they are no more."*

—MATTHEW 2:16–18

Since I was a young child, I have always loved words—their meanings, histories, etymologies. Sometimes opening a dictionary reveals an entire story—an entire universe, even—beneath a single word.

One word I've gotten to know recently is the Greek term *chora* (χώρα). It surfaces often in Orthodox iconography and hymnography in reference to the Theotokos, and it has two interrelated meanings. Most often, it refers to an open space or field, usually a way of conveying Mary's virginity. Comparisons of her womb to an unplowed, unsown field are plentiful in the countless *theotokia* and other hymns of the Orthodox tradition. But a chora can also be a container, vessel, or receptacle, as in the epithet Container of the Uncontainable (Χώρα του Αχωρήτου), which can sometimes be found alongside the Mother of God in icons or hymns.

It is this second sense of *chora* that has most captured my imagination. The uncontainable reality she contains is, of course, the living God. The idea of Mary-as-vessel identifies her as the living fulfillment of Old Testament sacred vessels like the ark of the covenant or the temple itself—inanimate objects that housed the presence of God. "In this way," writes Sotiria Kordi, "the figure of the Virgin attains a spatial dimension that is akin to an unusual space, a space with extraordinary characteristics. . . . The Virgin Chora is a bridge between the human and the divine, a mother and a receptacle for the Uncontainable."[20]

*Container of the Uncontainable.* When I hear this phrase, I think not only of the uncontainable God, but also of uncontainable grief. I think of how the Theotokos did not just bear God in the sense of containing Him; she also bore Him in the sense that she endured His grief, His heartbroken love for the creatures He was seeking to save. I think of the tears she would shed for her Son as He struggled for breath on the Cross, and I think of the innumerable generations of grief and sin that necessitated His Birth and death in the first place. I think of the weeping of Rachel, the breathless sobs of a mother trying to bear the unbearable, and of the Theotokos as God's loving response to that lamentation.

And I think of the Holy Innocents—the first martyrs of the Christian record—who did not even live long enough to properly bear witness to Him for whose sake they were slaughtered. It is but one episode in the long tragedy of human history, one contraction in the birth pangs with which "the whole creation groans and labors . . . together until now" (Rom. 8:22). And yet this event is somehow the saddest, most senseless type of sin—a ruler willing to snuff out a multitude of tiny, defenseless lives in a last-ditch effort to preserve his power.

It is tempting to gloss over this commemoration, to jump to the "happy ending" or, rather, happy beginning of Christ's Birth and what it would accomplish for mankind.

But if Mary was, as Fr. Thomas Hopko relished pointing out, "the great example, not the great exception," then let us try to follow in her footsteps in these Nativity feasts of lament. Let us seek to contain the uncontainable God within us, including bearing His unbearable grief. Sometimes this may mean learning to see suffering through His eyes of self-emptying love and care; other times it may mean responding to sin with grief, humility, repentance, or courage rather than despair. But always, it means bearing witness to suffering—endeavoring to see and offer up the world's brokenness (and our own) to God, rather than turning away or insulating ourselves from it.

*The iniquitous one, seeking the hidden Treasure,*
*slew the innocent babes on this day;*
*and Rachel was inconsolable,*

*beholding their unjust slaughter and untimely death,*
*and wept for them, her womb wracked with pain.*
*But she is gladdened now, seeing them*
*in the bosom of Abraham.*

—VESPERS FOR DECEMBER 29

# The Telos of Pain

### NICOLE M. ROCCAS

*He Himself likewise shared in [flesh and blood], that through death He might destroy him who had the power of death, that is, the devil, and release those who through fear of death were all their lifetime subject to bondage. . . . Therefore, in all things He had to be made like His brethren, that He might be a merciful and faithful High Priest in things pertaining to God, to make propitiation for the sins of the people. For in that He Himself has suffered, being tempted, He is able to aid those who are tempted.*

—HEBREWS 2:14–15, 17–18

Today's verses speak of Christ's willingness to take on human form—with all its pain and decay—in order to atone for our sins. He entered our bodily and existential condition from the inside out, in order to elevate us above the bondage of death. Saint Athanasius puts it this way: "He was made man that we might be made God; and He manifested Himself by a body that we might receive the idea of the unseen Father; and He endured the insolence of men that we might inherit immortality."[21]

In other words, in Christ's life, suffering, death, and Resurrection, "He became what we are," to borrow the classic formulation of St. Irenaeus, and in doing so blazed a redemptive trail through our own suffering.

I often wonder why. Why go through all the agony of having a human body? Why put Himself through the frustrations of the flesh, the torment of the Cross, just for us?

A friend asked me a similar question the other day. "You don't have to do this," she reminded me. "If you know it's going to be so painful, why bother?"

The "it" in question was the 26.2-mile marathon I had signed up to run a few days after our conversation.

Despite six months of consistent training, and despite the fact I've run a marathon before, I was pretty anxious. I knew it would hurt—*a lot*. I knew that around mile twenty, I would hit the notorious "wall," the personal abyss all marathon runners know about, when I would have to fight the primal urge to crawl, sob, or throw a temper tantrum in the middle of the course. The experience is a kind of total pain pressing in on the whole self—body, mind, and soul.

I knew all this. And frankly, I was terrified.

Hence my friend's question: *If you know it's going to be so painful, why bother?*

Short answer: *Because* it's so painful.

The pain is what scared me, but it's also a marker of how the race would be good for me. It's what tells me there is a weakness in need of strengthening, a mountain in need of summiting, fears in need of mastering. Without the pain, it wouldn't seem as if anything was at stake, at least not enough to warrant spending so much time and energy in training for half a year. It's what makes a marathon feel like a marathon and the finish line feel like the finish line.

Pain isn't enjoyable for its own sake but for the *telos*—the aim or end purpose—it points to: the joy of crossing the finish line, of completing a long training journey through the deserts of fear, tight hamstrings, and weak knees; crossing the Jordan River of a long race; and finally arriving on the shores of a land flowing with . . . Well, the thought of milk and honey right after a marathon is a little nauseating, so I'll say bagels and a beer.

To be clear: the distress of running a marathon is only a shadow—maybe less than that—of the agony Christ endured on the Cross, not to mention His descent into hell itself. Likewise, finishing a race hardly compares to Christ's accomplishment in destroying death.

Still, I think of Christ praying in the Garden of Gethsemane, supplicating for a way around the agony He knew awaited Him. I think of His drowsy disciples. I think of how Christ might have responded if one of them, instead of sleeping, had turned to Him and asked what my own friend asked me the other day.

*If you know it's going to be so painful, why bother?*

I don't know how Christ would have responded, but in the saving events of His death and Resurrection, pain was not the deciding factor. In dying on the Cross, Christ did not seek pain in itself, as some of us might in order to somehow "prove" ourselves in human terms. Yet neither did He seek to avoid pain. He sought only to conquer death, to save humanity, and was willing to take on whatever was required to accomplish that. He didn't turn away from death, because He could see past the tortures of the journey to the end—the Resurrection, life eternal, a new creation.

> *Beholding that which He had created*
> *according to His image and likeness*
> *corrupted by disobedience,*
> *Jesus descended, bowing down the heavens,*
> *and made His abode in the Virgin's womb*
> *without undergoing change,*
> *that in her He might restore Adam, who*
> *had become corrupt, yet cries:*
> *Glory to Your appearance, O my Deliverer and God!*
> —VESPERS FOR DECEMBER 25

# Death–Life Experiences

### NICOLE M. ROCCAS

*In Him you were also circumcised with the circumcision made without hands, by putting off the body of the sins of the flesh, by the circumcision of Christ, buried with Him in baptism, in which you also were raised with Him through faith in the working of God, who raised Him from the dead. And you, being dead in your trespasses and the uncircumcision of your flesh, He has made alive together with Him, having forgiven you all trespasses.*

—COLOSSIANS 2:11–13

In an essay on the mystery of death in the Orthodox Church, Metropolitan Kallistos Ware draws readers to what he calls "death-life experiences."[22] These forms of death, whether literal or metaphorical, are common to the human condition and ultimately serve a creative rather than destructive function. The death of our childhood, for example, is one such death-life experience: "Something in us has to die so that we may pass on to the next stage of living," he writes. A causality is at work between death of the old and life of the new in events like getting married, having children, or moving away from familiar surroundings. Even experiences typically regarded as painful—such as facing rejection or even wrestling with doubt—can bring about growth and a fuller awareness of life.

For Metropolitan Kallistos, recognizing our own death-life experiences can help us better understand our lives in the context of the saving events in Christ's life:

> The constantly repeated pattern of death-resurrection within our own lives is given fuller meaning by the life, death and Resurrection of our Savior Jesus Christ.... Our little deaths and resurrections are joined across history to His definite death and Resurrection; our little passovers are taken up and reaffirmed in His great passover.[23]

Through this lens, we can begin to perceive the many experiences that have shaped us, whether pleasant or painful, as landmarks orienting us toward the life-creating death of Christ. We can begin this process by considering what lies before us today, as we anticipate tomorrow's Feast of Christ's Circumcision and, for those following the New Calendar, the start of a new year. Both events fall into Metropolitan Kallistos's category of "death-life experiences." They both involve the dying of something old and the entrance or manifestation of something new.

In the case of His circumcision, Christ's submission to the law is a kind of death, a humiliation, a foreshadowing of the blood He will shed on the Cross. And yet by completing and fulfilling the Old Covenant, His circumcision is also a death-life experience. It is a call for us to die—not as in the old, physical circumcision, but in the new, spiritual one—so that we, and all our bodily and spiritual members, might find life in the fullest sense. While we were once "dead in [our] trespasses and the uncircumcision of [our] flesh," as St. Paul wrote to the Colossians, Christ has, in His circumcision, "made [us] alive together with Him" (Col. 2:13).

The start of a new year on January 1, although not a liturgical commemoration, can also be seen as an annual death-life experience. There is something about a new year that, regardless of our spiritual proclivities, awakens our longing to be free from old, deadening, destructive patterns of being. Whether we formulate New Year's resolutions or not, the simple act of starting a new calendar or writing the new year's numerals for the first time is often enough to spark that mysterious synergy of awe, hope, and regret. We see perhaps with greater clarity than at any other time the ways we have missed the mark—over the course of the past year or of our entire lives—and our longing to lead a life of meaning, fullness, and love. But to enter into that kind of life, we know there will be struggle in the form of dying to our usual, stale way of being in the world. Will we be faithful in that struggle, or will we be standing in the same place next year, caught in the same crosshairs of renewed hope and existential anguish?

Thank God that, however faithfully we have managed to navigate the countless death-life experiences of our year and our lives, it is Christ—not we or our own good intentions—who has made us "alive together with Him, having forgiven . . . all trespasses" (Col. 2:13).

*Having been granted the longed-for experience*
*of the Advent of God, the Christ-pleasing people*
*tearfully pray to see the regeneration, the life-giving Baptism.*
*All-pure and holy Virgin, grant us the*
*favor to venerate that glory.*
—MATINS FOR DECEMBER 31

# The Torah Is Now Being Fulfilled

### FR. STEPHEN DE YOUNG

*And when the parents brought in the Child Jesus, to do for
Him according to the custom of the law, [Simeon] took Him
up in his arms and blessed God and said:*

> *"Lord, now You are letting Your servant depart in peace,*
> *According to Your word;*
> *For my eyes have seen Your salvation*
> *Which You have prepared before the face of all peoples,*
> *A light to bring revelation to the Gentiles,*
> *And the glory of Your people Israel."*

—LUKE 2:27B–32

The Torah, the Law, was given to Moses for a particular
purpose. This Law, as recorded in the first five books of
the Old Testament, was never meant to last forever; the Torah
was never an end in itself. The Law was never a list of rules for
people to follow in order to "be saved" or "go to heaven." It was
given, according to the troparion below, by Christ Himself to
His own people in ancient times.

When, through Moses, God brought His people out of
Egypt and formed them into the nation of Israel, He desired
to live with them. God has never needed human persons, or

anything else for that matter. Rather, out of His abundant love, He has chosen to create beings with whom to share His divine and eternal life. This is not just hypothetical; it is real. God loved and desired to share Himself with a motley collection of late-Bronze-Age migrant workers and slaves, and he brought a terrible judgment against Egypt and her spiritual and political rulers in order to free His people and make this possible.

Though God's love for His newborn nation of Israel was pure, the reverse was not the case. Humans then as now are sinful, selfish, petty, quick to anger, and slow to forgive. For God to live among a sinful, wicked group of people was dangerous—not for God, but for His people. His holiness can be harmful to the wicked, and in the Old Testament, some even died from touching the ark of the covenant or otherwise coming into contact with God unworthily.

The Torah was given to manage this problem, though the Law by itself was powerless to solve it. Through the sacrifices commanded in the Torah, the people of Israel could be cleansed of sin and its effects. By keeping the commandments, Israelites could avoid sin in the first place and live lives of purity and holiness. In structuring their society as God directed them, they could live their lives together as a nation with their God in a way that would bring blessing rather than curse. Had Israel followed the Law, she would have been a beacon of light to the other nations of the world to draw them to worship Israel's God.

Unfortunately, as the Old Testament recounts, Israel neglected the commandments at all levels. Even the southern tribes and the kingdom of Judah, the more faithful elements in Israelite history, fell into idolatry, immorality, and corruption.

Rather than being a beacon of light to foreign, pagan nations, Israel and Judah became like those other nations and, in some cases, even worse. Ultimately, because of the unrepentant sin of His people, God had to depart from the temple and give up dwelling with them for their own protection.

The Torah, however, was not God's last word regarding the problem of human sin and wickedness. It was a stopgap for God's people, the people from whom the Messiah, the Christ, would ultimately come. Today, as we celebrate Christ taking upon Himself circumcision, the symbol of the practice of the Law, a radical change is taking place—a change to which St. Simeon bore witness. The Torah is now being fulfilled. The problem it served to manage is now being solved. The Law is no longer needed as a caretaker.

God has come to dwell among His people forever in the Person of Jesus Christ. He will never have to depart, because He purifies us perfectly from our sins with His own blood. Christ has rebuilt the fallen tent of David into His Church, the eternal people of God (Amos 9:11; Acts 15:16). We no longer need to be afraid of the holiness of God, because we have all been made holy by our Lord and God and Savior Jesus Christ (Col. 2:11). Now we are free to experience His holiness as love and light and life.

*Today is Christ carried into the sanctuary as a babe;*
*today does He become subject to the Law*
*who gave the law to Moses!*
*The armies of the angels marveled,*
*beholding Him who holds all things*

*borne in the arms of an elderly man.*
*And, full of reverence, Simeon cried out, rejoicing:*
*"Now let me depart from this fleeting life to*
*a rest which waxes not old, O Savior;*
*for I have seen Thee and am glad!"*
—GREAT VESPERS FOR JANUARY I

# The Line That Runs through Our Own Hearts

FR. STEPHEN DE YOUNG

*"I indeed baptize you with water unto repentance, but He who is coming after me is mightier than I, whose sandals I am not worthy to carry. He will baptize you with the Holy Spirit and fire. His winnowing fan is in His hand, and He will thoroughly clean out His threshing floor, and gather His wheat into the barn; but He will burn up the chaff with unquenchable fire."*
—MATTHEW 3:11–12

Saint John the Forerunner's preaching doesn't look much like anything we're used to hearing in church. Most preaching that we hear on a regular Sunday morning is concerned with teaching the gospel, explaining and advising how to live the Christian life, and calling for repentance from sin, which will bring forgiveness and healing. Other than some fringe groups that often become the focus of the media, Christian preaching and evangelization outside of churches, in public and to the public, focuses on the promise of the gospel and the meaning and fulfillment to be found in Christ. Though, like all human endeavors, our preaching is always flawed, partial, and unbalanced, we aim at proclaiming a positive message.

What St. John the Forerunner proclaimed throughout his public ministry, however, as recorded in the Gospels, is focused on judgment. He warned that the axe was at the root of the tree (Matt. 3:10). He excoriated those who came to him for baptism, asking who it was who warned them to flee from the coming wrath (Matt. 3:7; Luke 3:7). He spoke of a harvest and a division, warning that the unworthy would be burned with unquenchable fire. The ideas of God's wrath and His judgment coming upon the earth are, to most of us, profoundly negative images. We are uncomfortable with them and certainly would not lead off our outreach to the world by proclaiming them.

We must remember, however, that we live in profoundly different circumstances from those in St. John's audience. The Judeans who came to hear and in many cases be baptized by him had for centuries suffered brutal domination by foreign empires. Beginning with the Babylonians, who had taken them into exile, followed by the Persians, the Greeks, and finally the Romans, Judeans were controlled and all but enslaved by foreign masters. The Roman Empire's tyranny over Judea was not simply political—there was no separation of politics from religion or personal life in the ancient world. The Romans controlled when and how Judeans could worship, what they could eat, how they could dress, where they could travel, their business dealings, family life, and every other element of the way of life given to them in the Torah.

For these oppressed Judeans, then, the idea of God coming to judge and reveal His wrath was not a threat but a promise. They yearned for the day when He would bring justice against their enemies and for them in their suffering. The prominent party of the Pharisees gave extensive rulings on what must be done so that when that day of vengeance came, one could be numbered among the righteous who would be vindicated rather than the wicked who would suffer.

Saint John proclaimed to Judea their hope, but not in a hopeful way. He preached that it was not the Romans who would be judged immediately, but the Judean people who would first be sifted like wheat and purified. The Pharisees rejected his teaching for precisely this reason: he accused them of being sinners rather than acknowledging their righteousness, and he warned them to repent before it was too late.

As we near the end of our celebration of Christ's first coming, we also remember that He will come again. As we do so, St. John speaks to us the same word that he spoke so long ago: He warns us that the line between good and evil does not separate us from our enemies. Christ's judgment will not divide the "good people" who are like us from those bad people out there. God is not coming to vindicate churchgoing Christians and punish outsiders.

Rather, the line of judgment runs through the center of our own heart and soul and mind. This division runs through our communities, our families, and our selves. There is in each of us a mixture of crops and weeds, of wheat and of chaff. Each day God gives us an opportunity to repent and to weed the gardens of our lives. He calls on us each day to judge ourselves now so that we will not be judged then, when we meet our Lord Jesus Christ (1 Cor. 11:31). For this reason, we examine our lives and our hearts to become the person God created each of us to be.

*Let us piously sound forth beforehand*
*the hymns of the forefeast of the honored baptism of our God;*
*for, lo! as a man He wishes to approach*
*His Forerunner in the flesh*
*and to request saving baptism for the*
*edification of all that with faith*
*are enlightened in sacred manner and partake of the Spirit.*
—VESPERS FOR JANUARY 2

# Christ Purifies Everything He Touches

## FR. STEPHEN DE YOUNG

*Then Jesus came from Galilee to John at the Jordan to be baptized by him. And John tried to prevent Him, saying, "I need to be baptized by You, and are You coming to me?" But Jesus answered and said to him, "Permit it to be so now, for thus it is fitting for us to fulfill all righteousness." Then he allowed Him.*

—MATTHEW 3:13–15

Baptism, as preached and practiced by St. John the Forerunner, was not a completely new thing in Judea. John's practice of the baptism of repentance for the remission of sins, and eventually Christian baptism, certainly have a unique character. The Judean people who originally heard the Forerunner's preaching at the Jordan, however, had a framework in which to understand what he was doing and what baptism meant.

The most important key to understanding baptism is the concept of uncleanness in the Torah. Sometimes we confuse uncleanness in the Old Testament with sin, but these are two different categories. Many of the things that made someone unclean were not innately sinful but were matters of what we now call hygiene. Using the restroom and other biological processes made a person unclean. Touching a dead body, even to bury a loved one, made someone unclean. Coming into contact with someone who had certain sicknesses in order to care for them also made a person unclean.

The proper response for someone who had become unclean was not to repent, but to be washed. A whole series of ritual washings and baths existed within Judaism during St. John's time. These washings removed this state of uncleanness and allowed people to reenter their day-to-day lives without potentially making others unclean as well. Archaeologists have uncovered large communal baths that pilgrims to Jerusalem used before they entered the temple's courts.

But committing sins also made someone unclean. In addition to the sin itself, this uncleanness was addressed through the sacrifices at the temple in Jerusalem. Certain sins required the unclean person to make sacrifices as well as restitution to the person who was wronged. Someone who stole was required to repay what he had taken. Someone who gave false testimony in a trial received the penalty that would have been meted out to the person they testified against. After the sins were dealt with through repentance, sacrifice, and restitution, the guilty person would wash, to be cleansed of past sins and to make a new start.

Likewise, when the people came to St. John the Forerunner to be baptized, he warned them of the coming judgment in dire terms. They then confessed their sins in order to receive forgiveness. The washing of baptism in the Jordan rendered them clean, allowing them to begin again and to make a new start (Matt. 3:6). But the Pharisees did not think they needed the baptism of John because they believed they were already pure (Luke 7:30).

When Jesus came to St. John to be baptized, His forerunner immediately protested. Christ is without sin and so did not need any repentance or forgiveness. He had nothing to confess while John baptized Him. Jesus is clean, pure, and holy; He has no uncleanness that needs to be removed. Christ was beginning His public preaching ministry, but He did not need to start over and make a new beginning. He was merely revealing Himself publicly before the people of Galilee and Judea.

Because our Lord Jesus Christ is God Himself, when He touches something unclean, He does not Himself become unclean. Rather, that which was unclean becomes clean at the touch of Christ, whether from the uncleanness of leprosy and other diseases or from the uncleanness that results from sin. When Christ was baptized, He purified the waters; the waters did not purify Him. The Baptism of Christ is the beginning of the purification and salvation of the world. When He became man, Christ purified our human nature. When He was baptized, He purified the water. Through His death and Resurrection, He has purified and transfigured the world. By bringing the love of Christ into every part of our lives and hearts, every part of us can become clean and new and whole again.

*When he beheld You approaching and*
*asking to be baptized by him,*
*Your forerunner, O Lord, cried out with fear:*
*"O my God, my Creator, how can I*
*baptize You, who are undefiled?"*
—VESPERS FOR JANUARY 3

# Unknown Yet Important

FR. STEPHEN DE YOUNG

*After these things the Lord appointed seventy others also, and sent them two by two before His face into every city and place where He Himself was about to go. Then He said to them, "The harvest truly is great, but the laborers are few; therefore pray the Lord of the harvest to send out laborers into His harvest. Go your way; behold, I send you out as lambs among wolves."*

—LUKE 10:1–3

If we read the Gospels and the Acts of the Apostles closely, we see that Christ's followers, both during His earthly ministry and immediately thereafter, were not disorganized. They were not just a ragtag group following a charismatic leader. Within the larger group of followers, everyone recognized positions of relative authority and leadership. They did all things in an orderly fashion. Likewise, the various leadership positions we see in the Church today are not structures that evolved over time, created by men in a quest for power or control, but are extensions of that original good order.

Most people are familiar with the twelve disciples who were Christ's closest followers during His earthly ministry. The Gospels describe the calling of the Twelve and many of Christ's interactions with them, individually and as a group. Within this group, three disciples in particular formed a sort of inner circle of Christ's ministry: Ss. Peter, James, and John. Jesus chose to take these three with Him to witness important moments such as the Transfiguration and His raising of the dead.

Later, St. Paul will refer to Peter, James, and John as "pillars" of the Church (Gal. 2:9). Various forms of Judaism at the time referred to Abraham, Isaac, and Jacob as the pillars of Israel. The parallel between these three great apostles and the three great patriarchs of Genesis fits well with the number of the disciples in general. The twelve disciples parallel the twelve sons of Jacob who lent their names to the twelve tribes of Israel in the Old Testament.

While these saints and first followers of Christ are well known, the Scriptures speak much less about another group presented in the Gospels. This group of followers is known as the seventy apostles, or just the Seventy. Scripture does not contain a list of their names, though they are found very early in Christian tradition. Based on these lists, we can see that many of the followers of Christ mentioned in the Gospels and Acts, beyond the Twelve and St. Paul, are members of this larger group.

The number seventy is very important in Old Testament traditions. In Genesis 10, seventy nations make up the world outside Israel. When Moses needs help governing the affairs of the newborn people of God, he appoints seventy elders (Num. 11:16–17). Seventy elders made up the government of Israel and later Judea, and this number became traditional. The Sanhedrin, as encountered in the Gospels and Acts, was made up of seventy religious elders who governed Judea's affairs.

Christ's seventy disciples and the seventy elders in the next generation of the early Church stand in both these traditions. Throughout the Roman world, the Seventy held positions of leadership in various Christian communities that they had established as missionaries. As apostles, those "sent out" by Christ, they brought the gospel to the seventy nations, baptizing them and making disciples (Matt. 28:19). The Seventy were both leaders of the renewed Israel, the Church, and witnesses to the nations concerning Jesus the Christ.

Though the Scriptures speak less of the Seventy as a group than of Christ's inner circle of disciples, they are far from unimportant. When Christ sent them out during His earthly ministry, He anticipated the role they would play in baptizing disciples from all nations. When He called the Seventy in addition to the Twelve, He demonstrated that He is the Savior not only of the tribes of Israel but also of all the nations of the world. Several different Orthodox sources list the Seventy, but despite their importance in the early Church, in most cases, all we know about them is their names. Some of their names are mentioned in the Bible, and some of them only in these lists. But all of them, whether famous or unknown, are saints who served God in their lives and were leaders in Christ's Church. Their reward is not fame or notoriety but eternal life with Christ and all His saints.

*Elucidating the mysteries, the Wisdom*
*of God summons to the light*
*all among the nations who before lay in*
*the lightless darkness of ignorance,*

*leading them up to knowledge of the truth*
*and to the light through baptism,*
*which cleanses men's hearts and edifies*
*them through the Spirit.*
—COMPLINE FOR JANUARY 4

# Never Too Late to Begin Again

### FR. STEPHEN DE YOUNG

*What shall we say then? Shall we continue in sin that grace may abound? Certainly not! How shall we who died to sin live any longer in it? Or do you not know that as many of us as were baptized into Christ Jesus were baptized into His death? Therefore we were buried with Him through baptism into death, that just as Christ was raised from the dead by the glory of the Father, even so we also should walk in newness of life.*

—ROMANS 6:1–4

No matter how unclean or corrupted something has become, when it is thoroughly washed it is made clean again. A plate or cup may have sat in a cupboard or a box gathering dust. It may have been abandoned in a sink. It may have become so filthy that no one would want to touch it, let alone eat or drink from it. But if that same plate or cup is washed with detergent and hot water, it can find a whole new use, and its former state is quickly forgotten.

Rather than paying large sums of money for purebred animals, people today often adopt pets from a shelter. These animals, most of them abandoned dogs and cats, are frequently malnourished and scared, with visible ribs, wiry hair, and physical shaking giving tangible form to their neglect and suffering.

Often, however, once a human family adopts one of these animals into a loving and caring home, the new pet not only physically blossoms and looks like a whole new creature, but it also begins to take on a new personality and the characteristics of its owners.

Both the dirty cup and the neglected animal can be helpful metaphors for understanding baptism. Holy Baptism is more than just the washing of the body, but this washing—being purified from uncleanness and the residue of the past—is a clear analogy for what is happening spiritually. And when we are baptized, we are adopted into the household and family of God. Just as an adopted dog or cat starts to behave in ways that are like its human family, so also when we spend time with Christ and His family, we begin to become more like Him.

In the Scripture reading for today, St. Paul writes about baptism in an even more radical way: the person we were before baptism is dead; now, in Christ, each of us is a whole, newly created person. All our past sins were committed by someone else; we have a new and fresh start.

The Fathers tell us that we can attain a new identity not only in our baptism. They compare tears of repentance to a "second baptism." The door for us to make a new start is always open when we return to Christ in repentance and confession. Every moment God gives us is an opportunity for repentance and healing. We are able to break character. Who we were in the past does not need to be who we are today—or who we will be tomorrow. As long as we live, it is never too late for any of us to begin again by laying aside old sins and being purified and given new life from our Lord and God and Savior Jesus Christ.

*You make souls new through the Spirit,*
*and by water sanctify their body,*
*which is composed of diverse parts,*
*building up the life of man;*
*for as the Physician of souls and bodies, with wise forethought*
*You apply the remedy which each part requires.*
—COMPLINE FOR JANUARY 5

# Jesus Reveals the Holy Trinity to Us

### FR. STEPHEN DE YOUNG

*When He had been baptized, Jesus came up immediately from the water; and behold, the heavens were opened to Him, and He saw the Spirit of God descending like a dove and alighting upon Him. And suddenly a voice came from heaven, saying, "This is My beloved Son, in whom I am well pleased."*

—MATTHEW 3:16–17

The God who created the universe has always been and will always be a Holy Trinity of Persons. God, His Word, and His Spirit appear throughout the Old Testament, even from the first page. Throughout the history of God's people Israel, and later Judah and Judea, God revealed Himself to humanity, formed relationships with them, dwelt among them, and even, as in the case of Abraham, ate with them. The teaching of the Holy Trinity is not a change in the New Testament. The Holy Trinity is not an idea invented by early Christians or at church councils.

What changes in the New Testament, expressed particularly at Christ's Baptism at the hand of St. John the Forerunner in the Jordan, is that the Holy Trinity comes to be known fully through Jesus Christ. In the Old Testament, we see glimpses everywhere, and Jewish scholars before the Birth of Christ had even begun to put these pieces together. These Jewish scholars, before Christianity had come to exist, saw a distinction between God and His Spirit, even as they saw that the Spirit is not other than God Himself. They also saw a figure called by many different names in the Hebrew Scriptures: the Word, the Son of Man, the Angel of the Lord, and still other names. This person who appeared in their holy writings was distinguished from God but also was identified as being God.

At the very beginning of Genesis, we see God creating the heavens and the earth (Gen. 1:1). The Spirit of God hovers over the waters (v. 2). God speaks His Word and through the Word; He creates all things (vv. 3ff). In the day of Israel's birth as a people, Moses and the people of God stood at the shore of the sea. Pharaoh and his vengeful armies made haste to catch and destroy them before they could make their Exodus complete. While Moses heard from God how He would save His people, the Angel of the Lord who led Israel and the pillar of cloud that went before them moved and took up a position behind Israel, between them and the Egyptians, to protect them (Ex. 14:19).

These hints, shadows, and tantalizing details preserved in the Scriptures were enough to give attentive Jewish scholars an understanding of their God, but from a distance. The details were uncertain, and all sorts of religious scribes proposed different ideas about how God's Word and His Spirit related to God Himself. No one on earth before the Birth of Christ could claim to truly understand the God whom they worshipped.

But God did not want to be unknowable. He created humanity to know Him and to be known by Him. But being creatures, we have no way to understand our Creator. Everything that we know and understand, we know only about other created things like us. We even struggle to fully comprehend other created things. God is not even *like* anything we know on earth. All of our analogies and comparisons for the Holy Trinity ultimately fall apart and fail.

This all changed when God became man in the Person of Jesus Christ. Christ took up our human nature; He made Himself as we are. Because of this, we can come to know Him as a Person. We can understand who He is. We can follow Him. We can become like Him because He became like us. As we come to know Him, we also come to know His Father. As we come to know Him, He gives us His Spirit. Through Christ we come to know God, and God shares His life with us. His life lasts forever.

Only two of the Gospels tell the story of the Birth of Jesus, but all four of them tell the story of Christ's Baptism. Christ became man for our salvation at His conception, but it was in the Jordan River with St. John that He revealed His identity as God to the world. The Baptism of Jesus was the beginning of Christ's earthly ministry and our salvation. His Baptism was also the moment when God the Holy Trinity was fully revealed to the whole world. All of humanity could now come to know their Creator. Coming to know who God is is not a subject for highly educated academics or wise sages. Knowing about God doesn't require mastering obscure Latin theology. By coming to know our Lord and God and Savior Jesus Christ, anyone and everyone can know God Himself.

*When our Deliverer was baptized by His servant*
*and borne witness to by the coming of the Holy Spirit,*
*the angelic armies, looking on, were stricken with awe;*
*and a voice was borne down from the Father in heaven:*
*"He whom the forerunner baptized with*
*his hand is My beloved Son,*
*in whom I have been well-pleased!"*
*O Christ our God, glory to You!*
—VESPERS OF HOLY THEOPHANY, JANUARY 6

# Greatness through Faithfulness

FR. STEPHEN DE YOUNG

*"He who has the bride is the bridegroom; but the friend of
the bridegroom, who stands and hears him, rejoices greatly
because of the bridegroom's voice. Therefore this joy of mine is
fulfilled. He must increase, but I must decrease."*

—JOHN 3:29–30

Saint John the Baptist, or Forerunner, is all too often
neglected in our practice of the Orthodox Christian Faith.
In a certain way, this makes sense. Of all the saints, John was
called to a radical kind of humility. On this day, as we celebrate
his synaxis, or "liturgical assembly," we hear many great testimonies
to his character and mission and work. We hear that he
is the final seal of the Old Testament prophets. We hear that
he receives the greatest honor of all, to place his hand upon the
head of Christ at His Baptism. Christ Himself says that among
those born of women, none is greater than St. John (Matt.
11:11; Luke 7:28).

At the same time, however, Christ goes on to say that the
least in the Kingdom is greater than he. Saint John's life was

a difficult one cut all too short. His father was murdered by Herod's men as they sought to find and kill the newborn Messiah after Jesus' birth (Matt. 23:35). John's mother died not long after fleeing with her child to the wilderness, leaving him an orphan. He grew and came of age in the Judean desert with the angels as his companions and friends. He made his own clothes from knotty hair left on trees by camels scratching themselves. He lived on insects and other small desert creatures, as well as wild honey that he could find in the wilderness.

As an adult, St. John was sent on a prophetic mission. He was not sent to proclaim freedom, or deliverance, or salvation. Rather, the Baptist was sent to proclaim wrath, judgment, and repentance. While some came to baptism and the forgiveness of sins through this preaching, many rejected the Forerunner as a madman. We know that his enemies included the Pharisees, the temple authorities, and the Judean establishment in general. John's mission involved calling even Herod himself to repentance, though the result was not an opportunity to baptize the king but rather John's arrest, imprisonment, and ultimately execution. Through all these trials, the saint remained faithful to God, even to the point of death. After that death, he proclaimed the identity of Jesus as the Christ even in Hades, as the hymnography surrounding his beheading describes.

Despite remaining faithful to his calling throughout his life, St. John did not receive any honors in this world. He did not experience economic prosperity but lived in utmost poverty. He was not honored by kings and nobles but rather was murdered by them. He assembled a large following of disciples, but after doing so, God called him to send them away to follow Jesus instead. He lived the life of a servant—not of a master, or a leader, or a ruler.

Our culture has taught us that what counts at the end of our life in this world is success. In whatever we devote our lives to, we gauge success or failure in very materialistic terms. Were we respected members of our community? Did we advance to a high level in our chosen career? Did we ultimately accumulate wealth that enabled us to provide for ourselves and our children? Did we receive recognition from others for our skills, abilities, and hard work?

By all these standards, St. John was a failure. He owned essentially nothing. He never married nor had any children. More people despised and rejected him than respected him. After an extended imprisonment, his life ended in a vicious murder. Yet the Lord Jesus Christ, the one who is the sole judge of the living and the dead, assessed St. John, based on his life, as being truly great. Traditionally in iconography, he is the one who stands at the left hand of Christ's heavenly throne. The Forerunner is great because he was faithful. He was faithful to God from his birth through his unjust death. He served as he was called to serve. He loved the Lord.

Most of all, St. John understood that he was not the main character of his own life. His was a life lived in service to his faithful Lord and God and Savior Jesus Christ. To be a servant means to answer the call of the Lord. A servant does not choose what he or she wants to do, would like to do, would find fulfilling, or considers comfortable. Christ's call to each of us is unique and different. A faithful janitor is greater in the sight of the Lord than a faithless king or bishop.

As we go forth from the light of Christ at the Feast of Theophany, let us seek out our calling and opportunities to serve Christ and His Church by serving each other and working faithfully together toward the Kingdom of God.

*From the ancient snares have we all been set loose,*
*and the teeth of the lions have been broken in their mouths.*
*Let us then rejoice with great joy and open wide our mouths,*
*weaving with words a sweet hymn to the Word,*
*which delights to bestow gifts upon us.*
—MATINS FOR JANUARY 7

# Notes

1. St. Gregory of Nyssa, *On the Making of Man*, trans. H.A. Wilson, in *Nicene and Post-Nicene Fathers, Second Series*, ed. Philip Schaff and Henry Wace, vol. 5 (Buffalo, NY: Christian Literature Publishing Co., 1893), XVI.18. Revised and edited for *New Advent* by Kevin Knight. http:/www.newadvent.org/fathers/2914.htm.

2. Robert J. Miller, ed., *The Complete Gospels: Annotated Scholars Version* (Sonoma, CA: Polebridge Press, 1994), 384–385.

3. *The Protoevangelium of James*, trans. Alexander Walker, in *Ante-Nicene Fathers*, ed. Alexander Roberts, James Donaldson, and A. Cleveland Coxe, vol. 8 (Buffalo, NY: Christian Literature Publishing Co., 1886), 7. Revised and edited for *New Advent* by Kevin Knight, 2021, https://www.newadvent.org/fathers/0847.htm.

4. See Megan Nutzman, "Mary in the Protevangelium of James: A Jewish Woman in the Temple?" *Greek, Roman, and Byzantine Studies* 53 (2013): 551–578.

5. Nicholas Costas, ed. and trans., *Proclus of Constantinople and the Cult of the Virgin in Late Antiquity: Homilies 1–5, Texts and Translations* (Boston: Brill, 2003), 226ff.

6. St. Philaret of Moscow, "On Obedience. The Annunciation," *Orthodox Christianity*, April 7, 2017, https://orthochristian.com/102471.html.

7. St. Isaac the Syrian, *The Ascetical Homilies of St. Isaac the Syrian* (Brookline, MA: Holy Transfiguration Monastery, 1985), 35.

8. St. Isaac the Syrian, 381.

9. St. John Chrysostom, *Homilies on the Gospel of Matthew*, trans. George Prevost and M.B. Riddle, in *Nicene and Post-Nicene Fathers: First Series*, ed. Philip Schaff, vol. 10 (Buffalo, NY: Christian Literature Publishing Co., 1888). Revised and edited for *New Advent* by Kevin Knight, 2021, http://www.newadvent.org/fathers/2001.htm.

10. St. Irenaeus, *Against Heresies*, trans. Alexander Roberts and William Rambaut, in *Ante-Nicene Fathers*, ed. Alexander Roberts, James

Donaldson, and A. Cleveland Coxe (Buffalo, NY: Christian Literature Publishing Co., 1886), III, 22:4. Revised and edited for *New Advent* by Kevin Knight, 2021, http://www.newadvent.org/fathers/0103322.htm.

11. St. Peter of Damaskos, "A Treasury of Divine Knowledge: The Fourth Stage of Contemplation," in *The Philokalia: The Complete Text*, ed. and trans. G. E. H. Palmer, Philip Sherrard, and Kallistos Ware, vol. 3 (New York: Faber and Faber, 1995), loc. 19369, Kindle.

12. St. Gregory of Sinai, "On the Commandments and Doctrines," in *The Philokalia: The Complete Text*, ed. and trans. G. E. H. Palmer, Philip Sherrard, and Kallistos Ware, vol. 4 (New York: Faber and Faber, 1998), loc. 29264, Kindle.

13. St. John of Damascus, in *On the Orthodox Faith: A New Translation of An Exact Exposition of the Orthodox Faith*, trans. Norman Russell (Yonkers, NY: St Vladimir's Seminary Press, 2022), 246.

14. Luigi Gambero, *Mary and the Fathers of the Church: The Blessed Virgin Mary in Patristic Thought* (San Francisco: Ignatius Press, 1999), 192.

15. St. Ignatius, *The Epistle of Ignatius to the Ephesians*, trans. Alexander Roberts and James Donaldson, in *Ante-Nicene Fathers*, ed. Alexander Roberts, James Donaldson, and A. Cleveland Coxe, vol. 1 (Buffalo, NY: Christian Literature Publishing Co., 1885), ch. 19. Revised and edited for *New Advent* by Kevin Knight, 2021, https://www.newadvent.org/fathers/0104.htm.

16. *The Protoevangelium of James*, trans. Alexander Walker, in *Ante-Nicene Fathers*, ed. Alexander Roberts, James Donaldson, and A. Cleveland Coxe, vol. 8 (Buffalo, NY: Christian Literature Publishing Co., 1886), 9. Revised and edited for *New Advent* by Kevin Knight, 2021, https://www.newadvent.org/fathers/0847.htm.

17. St. Athanasius, *On the Incarnation*, trans. Archibald Robertson, in *Nicene and Post-Nicene Fathers, Second Series*, ed. Philip Schaff and Henry Wace, vol. 4 (Buffalo, NY: Christian Literature Publishing Co., 1892), 9.1. Revised and edited for *New Advent* by Kevin Knight, http://www.newadvent.org/fathers/2802.htm.

18. St. Athanasius, 9.4.

19. James K. A. Smith, *How to Inhabit Time: Understanding the Past, Facing the Future, Living Faithfully Now* (Grand Rapids, MI: Brazos Press, 2022), 18.
20. "The Chora parekklesion as a space of becoming" (PhD diss., University of Leeds, 2014), 43.
21. St. Athanasius, 54.3.
22. Kallistos Ware, "'Go Joyfully': The Mystery of Death and Resurrection," in *The Inner Kingdom: Volume 1 of the Collected Works* (Crestwood, NY: St Vladimir's Seminary Press, 2000), 25–42.
23. Ware, 29.

# Contributors

**Fr. Basil Ross Aden**
Archpriest Basil Ross Aden writes the Ancient Faith blog *The Word of the Day*, a commentary on the lectionary's daily epistle readings. A community college teacher, Fr. Basil published a textbook on religious studies and continues to write on the Orthodox Faith and life. He and his wife Sandra split their time between Michigan and Arizona.

**Elissa Bjeletich Davis**
Elissa Bjeletich Davis has published several books with Ancient Faith Publishing (*In God's Hands, Blueprints for the Little Church, Tending the Garden of Our Hearts,* and *Welcoming the Christ Child*) and hosts the podcasts *Light Streams In, Everyday Orthodox, Tending the Garden of Our Hearts,* and *Raising Saints* on Ancient Faith Radio. She and her husband, Chris, live in a house full of kids near Austin, Texas.

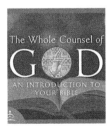

**Fr. Stephen De Young**
The V. Rev. Dr. Stephen De Young is the author of *Apocrypha, The Whole Counsel of God, God Is a Man of War,* and *The Religion of the Apostles* from Ancient Faith Publishing. He is the pastor of Archangel Gabriel

Orthodox Church (Antiochian) in Lafayette, Louisiana, and holds a PhD in biblical studies from Amridge University. He hosts the blog and podcast *The Whole Counsel of God* and cohosts the *Lord of Spirits* podcast on Ancient Faith Radio.

### Fr. Stephen Freeman

Father Stephen Freeman is an archpriest (OCA) and pastor emeritus of St. Anne Orthodox Church in Oak Ridge, Tennessee. He is the creator of the popular blog *Glory to God for All Things* and the weekly podcast *Glory to God* on Ancient Faith Radio, as well as the author of the Ancient Faith books *Face to Face: Knowing God Beyond Our Shame* and *Everywhere Present: Christianity in a One-Storey Universe*. His work has been widely translated and published in Europe and Russia.

### Fr. Michael Gillis

Father Michael Gillis is priest at Holy Nativity Orthodox Church in Langley, British Columbia, and author of the *Praying in the Rain* blog and podcast. He and his wife, Kh. Bonnie, live on a hobby farm and enjoy keeping chicken and geese and eating fresh greens from the garden. They have three daughters and eleven grandchildren.

### Laura S. Jansson

Laura S. Jansson is an Orthodox Christian doula, childbirth educator, and mother living and writing at the intersection of birth and faith. She earned her master's degree in theology and philosophy from the University of

Oxford and has guided scores of expectant mothers on the path to parenthood. Her Ancient Faith book *Fertile Ground: A Pilgrimage Through Pregnancy* is the first book for pregnant women arising from the Orthodox tradition.

### Nicole M. Roccas

Nicole M. Roccas, PhD, is a writer and certified trauma-informed coach who earned her PhD in history from the University of Cincinnati. She hosts the *Time Eternal* podcast and blog and is the author of three Ancient Faith books, including *Time and Despondency: Regaining the Present in Faith and Life*. She is based in Hamilton, Ontario. You can find her on Instagram (@nicoleroccas) or on her website (www.nicoleroccas.com).

### Brandi Willis Schreiber

Brandi Willis Schreiber is the author of poetry, prize-winning fiction, and nonfiction, including *A Long Walk with Mary: A Personal Search for the Mother of God* (AFP). A lover of beauty and words, she holds an MA and BA in English literature with emphases in creative writing and poetry, both from Texas Tech University. She attends St. Andrew Greek Orthodox Church in Lubbock, Texas, with her beloved family. Visit her at www.brandiwillisschreiber.com.

We hope you have enjoyed and benefited from this book. Your financial support makes it possible to continue our nonprofit ministry both in print and online. Because the proceeds from our book sales only partially cover the costs of operating **Ancient Faith Publishing** and **Ancient Faith Radio**, we greatly appreciate the generosity of our readers and listeners. Donations are tax deductible and can be made at **www.ancientfaith.com.**

To view our other publications,
please visit our website: **store.ancientfaith.com**

 **ANCIENT FAITH RADIO**

Bringing you Orthodox Christian music, readings, prayers, teaching, and podcasts 24 hours a day since 2004 at
**www.ancientfaith.com**

Milton Keynes UK
Ingram Content Group UK Ltd.
UKHW041313111123
432394UK00004B/314